M000158846

Sailing Into Oblivion

The Solo Non-stop Voyage of the Mighty Sparrow

Jerome Rand

To my parents,

Jim and Irma

Author's Note

While I planned this voyage, I was questioned over and over "Why am I doing this?" I came up with a few answers that seemed to make sense to most people, but only after being caught completely off guard the first time I was asked. In reality, I have no great answer to explain why I did what I did. I can only offer that from the very beginning of my sailing life I have always tried to go as far as I could. Around an entire lake or across an ocean, each passage was a little further than the last.

This eventually would lead me to attempt a solo non-stop circumnavigation of my own. No records were attempted, no sponsorships were sought out and very few people were informed of my intentions. I honestly didn't think I had very good odds of success. And though I didn't exactly know why I was going, I set sail from Gloucester Massachusetts on October 3rd, 2017.

In the following pages, my goal was not only to tell the tale of my sea adventure, but to also invite the reader aboard my 1975 Westsail 32, Mighty Sparrow. The chapters titled "Ships Log", were taken directly from my daily journal entries. March 28th thru April 12th, 2018 was the time I was more afraid for my life than at any other point on the voyage. It was where I was one of, if not the most, isolated human on the planet. While enduring a world that seemed determined to erase my existence, under the dim light of a headlamp, I would lay in my bunk and write. "Ships Log" chapters contain the exact words of the lone sailor, hungry, cold, and scared, plunging beyond the point of no return and deeper into the grip of the Great Southern Ocean.

Mighty Sparrow

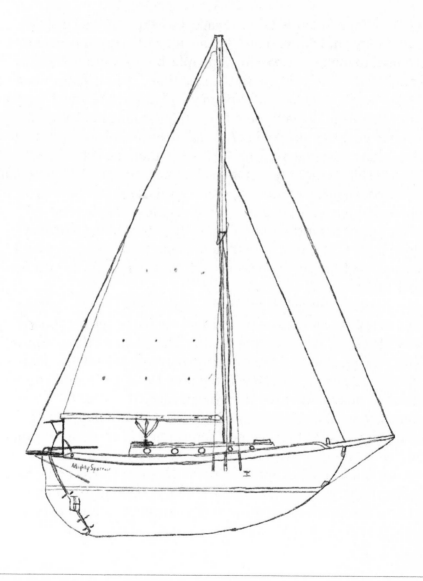

Beaufort Wind Force Scale:

F-1: (1-3knots) Light Air with little ripples on the sea surface

F-2: (4-6knots) Light Breeze with small wavelets

F-3: (7-10knots) Gentle Breeze with occasional wave crests

F-4 (11-16knots) Moderate Wind with frequent wave crests

F-5 (17-21knots) Fresh Breeze with moderate sized waves

F-6 (22-27knots) Strong Breeze with large waves

F-7 (28-33knots) Near Gale, large breaking waves and sea spray

F-8 (34-40knots) Gale, moderately high waves and breaking crests

F-9 (41-47knots) Severe Gale, high waves, sea spray affects visibility

F-10 (48-55knots) Storm, very high waves, long breaking crests

F-11 (56-63knots) Violent Storm, exceptional wave heights

F-12 (64Knots+) Hurricane force winds, survival conditions

Knots to mph conversion:

1 knot=1.14mph
Example; 11knots=12mph/55knots=63mph

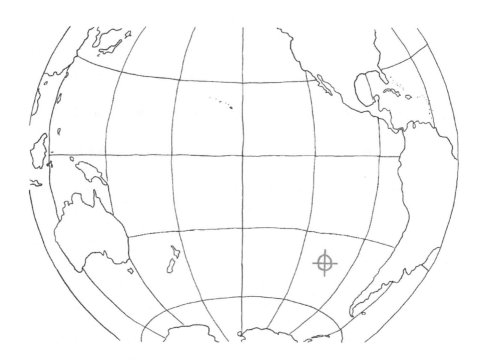

Chapter 1
Ships Log

0600 March 28th, 2018
Lat 48 45'S, Long 098 01'W
Miles from Cape Horn: 1,255
Days at Sea: 177

My hands are frozen again, I am trying to work the numb out of them using the stove right now. It's the only heat I feel in this place these days. It took about 30 minutes to scoop all of the hailstones from the last squall into a bucket to melt for drinking water. I'm down to less than 5 gallons of fresh water again and even though I am getting used to always needing water it is still a worry I can't escape from.

I wish I could use the neoprene gloves like I used to but the last time I tried to dry them with the stove it seems to have damaged the material and now little pieces of black rubber end up in the water and I can taste it, this can't be good to drink. So I just try to collect the snow and ice as fast as possible; for the sake of my hands and for the fact that just one wave can make the water unusable by contaminating the hail with salt.

Why on Earth am I here right now? I keep asking this question. Still so far from Cape Horn and yet I am in constant fear of what could happen tonight, tomorrow or next week. In reality I still have a month at the very least before I can sail North, out of the Southern Ocean and into the relative safety of the South Atlantic. It seems like a month has passed in the last 24 hours with all that has happened.

The knockdown last night will, no doubt, be forever in my mind. Not so much from the motion but from the noise. Asleep, ha, laying in my bunk, the dull rumble of passing waves is constant in this Gale. But around 2100 last night one just grew louder and louder until a very intense bang hit the boat with more force than I have ever felt. Like a truck slamming into the side of the boat we went over. This time much more violent and fast. I could only think for a second that the storage unit that Bob and I built, holding over 500 pounds of tools and gear is hanging above me and I hope it holds!

At the same time the rattle of 100 things flying from one side of the boat to the other as if shot from a gun. But what really alarmed me was the big bang on deck. I scramble to the hatch, not knowing what I might find, broken tiller, rudder, mast? Thankfully just the spray skirts and dodger were taken by the wave, I am very lucky once again.

Luck might not be the correct word here; I put myself in this terrible place so whatever happens is of my own doing. And what I have to do now is try to put up more sail on a raging sea in the hope that a moving target will be harder for the next wave to find. The winds have dropped from F-10 to F-8 and I think that might be why I was just knocked down. I am moving too slow for the conditions and the waves are what I am most worried about. The only sail I have set is the small Storm Jib, sheeted hard in the center to keep the Mighty Sparrow heading with the wind. So essentially, the pressure of the wind on the bare mast has been enough to keep us moving well; until now.

Chapter 2
One Adventure Leads to Another

July 13th, 2012
Mount Katahdin Maine
Day 133 hiking the Appalachian Trail

The descent back down the last 5 miles of the Appalachian Trail created some very wild emotions for me. Most hikers think of all the months of pain and suffering, the people they met and good times along the way. For me, it was the "checking off" of one adventure and the planning stage of the next. My Father, Jim, had come to Maine to hike the final mountain and share in the extraordinary experience that I had been having for the last 133 days. While we chatted about this and that, the gears in my head were spinning wildly.

What a feeling it was to be that guy, the one that took on the massive challenge to Thru Hike the Appalachian Trail, battled his way through 2,200 miles, and make it to the end. But these were not the thoughts that were bubbling up from my memory. What was coming to the surface had been sitting in the back of my mind for over 10 years. The Holy Grail of Sailing Adventures, a trip that could easily be put at the top of the toughest challenges in the world. Sail around the world, alone, and without stopping. I remember clearly wondering that if I felt this good finishing the AT after enduring more than 4 months in the woods, what would it be like to sail back into port after 9 months at sea?

Over the next few months I slowly morphed from Mountain Man to normal everyday life. A summer job, family, and friends. Northern Michigan is a great place to be in the summer but soon enough the snow would be falling, and I would need to make my way South. After 5 years in the Caribbean my resilience to the cold as a Michigander was all but gone. And as a sailor if you want to keep working you can't be sitting next to a frozen lake!

A big component in the early stages of my plan was money. I didn't have much and would need plenty. Enough to cover the cost of the boat, a year of sea trials, and then all of the supplies that would be needed for the actual trip. After a few months of searching and some odd jobs, a big piece of the puzzle fell into place. I was going back to the Bitter End Yacht Club. Returning to one of the best jobs I have ever had: Watersports Director.

This came with the advantage of onsite housing and food. I would be able to save almost everything that I could earn and still have more fun than almost anywhere else. I was also doing what I loved and had done for many years of my life. Just about the perfect fit for my plan. I figured three years would be enough time to save what was needed and, in the meantime, I would start looking for a suitable boat.

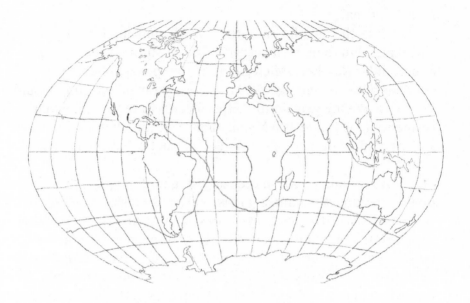

Chapter 3
The Game Plan

My introduction to non-stop Circumnavigating came in the books about the first attempts at sailing solo around the world non-stop in the 1968 Golden Globe Race. I settled for a traditional sail along the Clipper Ship route in a small world cruising boat. I figured my best chance of success would be in a boat from the 1970's. Something built as strong as a tank and able to bring me home safely, with the added bonus that I would be able to purchase one without breaking the bank.

My route would be a bit different than the majority of circumnavigations, most of which leave from Europe. I wanted to leave from an American Port and use the five Southern Capes as my waypoints. The Cape of Good Hope, Cape Leeuwen, South of Tasmania, Stewart Island New Zealand, and finally Cape Horn. Daunting when laid on a chart of the world but also a beautiful line when marked out. I spent many nights looking over the great oceans that spanned the three large charts I had purchased and kept close at hand for the years leading up to the trip.

The only other parameters I had for my circumnavigation were that I wanted to do this completely unsponsored and unassisted. After choosing Gloucester, Massachusetts as my port of departure, I had my passage plan set in stone. I intended to leave in the fall of 2017, sail south of the 5 Southern Capes, and return to Gloucester without sponsors, assistance, or ever putting down an anchor.

It should be noted that since learning to sail at the age of 18, I had crewed on boats sailing across the North Atlantic twice, South Atlantic once, and various other trips to and from the Caribbean. All together I had around 50,000 sea miles under my belt and a good understanding of what our ocean world was really like. I will admit that I have never tried my hand at any solo sailing outside of small boats in protected water. In some ways I was taking a big chance that solo sailing was something I might enjoy and more importantly something that I could even accomplish.

To sail alone at sea is a total communion between the sailor, the boat, and mother-nature. I can only say this now after doing so much of it. Before I cast off my lines on my first solo passage, I had no idea what I was getting into. Only the information I could glean from books written almost 50 year ago could give me an insight into the strange world of the Solo Sailor. What I did know was that it fascinated me. On the Appalachian Trail I spent the second half of the hike, about 75 days, mostly alone. The majority of other hikers having given up long before the halfway point. Both day and night were spent in solitude, my only interactions coming about once a week while resupplying in towns along the way. This trip was going to a whole new level as far as complete isolation. It is one thing to be able to walk a few miles to a road or town when you feel like it. I would be sailing in the middle of the largest open expanses on the planet. Thousands of square miles of ocean, void of anything but me and my boat.

Chapter 4
Ships Log

2200 March 29th, 2018
Lat 49 21' S, Long 095 44' W
Miles from Cape Horn: 1,105
Days at Sea: 178

The weather rages on for another day with the waves becoming very steep and providing some great surfing. Sparrow's bow drops and she takes off down each wave, everything vibrates, and then we quietly dig back into the water going from 15 down to 4 knots. One giant surf sent us sailing right into an uncontrolled Jibe! Back on deck as fast as I can to see if anything was broken, lucky again and everything seems fine in the darkness. Once back together and moving well I head down below to sit and think.

I am so sick of this place. The raging wind and seas, never knowing if the big wave is coming to get me. After the last knockdown I just can't get the sound of that wave out of my head. I hear more of them in the distance and can only hope that they don't find me. I wonder, if a person was dropped from land onto Sparrow right now just how long it would take them to go mad? I have become so used to this world of constant threat after so many months since the Cape of Good Hope, but it doesn't mean I am not scared as hell or that I like being here one bit!

Alas, we are making way so I can't complain too much. Day

by day Sparrow is putting miles in her wake and the line on my chart slowly crawls along this wet, tattered picture of the Pacific. Another big wave made its way over the stern and filled the cockpit. The force was enough to spray salt water into the cabin like a high-pressure hose, soaking my nav station again and adding to the overall wetness that is my world below deck. I am down to using the last few tank-top shirts to mop up both salt water from leaks and condensation drips on almost every surface.

The sound of dripping water from the engine room peaks my curiosity and I find the seal on the throttle box in the cockpit has gone and when the foot well fills with water it drips all over the engine! I will get some 5200 sealant on there as soon as I get the chance and then spray the engine with WD-40. I wish I had some more fresh water to rinse the salt off the engine; rust is everywhere. I wonder how long this has been going on?

Adding up some numbers, and by my calculation I hit 20,000 miles yesterday; only 1,000 miles until the Horn! Big numbers but the 5th Cape can't come soon enough. I flinch with every wave hit on Sparrow, hour after hour my nerves are shattered. I have been scared, cold, hungry and tired for too long. I just hope the next 10 days will go by without too many big problems. I have been spending most of my time pinned into my nav station just waiting and worrying. Waves are still breaking but the winds seem to be easing off. I will need to put up more sail but first I will try to get some sleep as the pressure is rising and things should ease up.

Chapter 5
Ready or Not

September 29th, 2017
Rockland Maine

No matter how much preparation and double checking is carried out on a boat, the true test begins when the keel gets wet. Sparrow had been out of the water for nearly 4 months but she was finally ready to go back into her element. Still held in the lift straps, I did the normal checks for water coming in from any fittings and all looked good. Giving Dave, the travel lift operator, a thumbs up I went to fire the engine and heard nothing but a thump! I know that sound; it was the sound of an engine that had water inside. I had run the engine a few days before to make sure this launch would go smoothly but somehow, even out of the water, she did it again. Whatever leftover water was in the exhaust system was now in the engine and had to be blown out.

A few frantic checks of other possibilities by Dave and me uncovered nothing. The fuel injectors had to come out to see if water truly had flooded the engine. Ten minutes later I had my answer; it was the water. Long story short, I pulled the 4 fuel injectors, cranked the engine, blew oil and water all over the clean engine room, changed the oil, replaced the injectors, and bled the fuel system. All good except I had cracked one of the rings that secured injector number three. My only solace in this moment was that it happened here on land! A few hours later and I had two spare injectors and replaced the broken one. I bled the fuel system once more and the engine fired right up! Not the best launch of the Mighty Sparrow under my watch but a launch nonetheless.

With Sparrow on the dock I had planned to do some of the heavy provisioning and a few other last-minute projects. The biggest of which was tuning the mast and rigging. My younger brother Adam would be flying into Portland Jetport around midnight to help with the overnight trip from Rockland to Gloucester. I was very tired from such a stressful day, not to mention the last month of knowing what I was about to embark upon. I spent many nights rolling around in my bunk while my mind raced through the boat preparation. Try as I might, at night I could never escape what I had gotten myself into; at this point there was no turning back.

Flying through a dark Maine night on the drive to pick up Adam, I was torn by being happy that he would help with the sail to Gloucester and annoyed that I wasn't on the boat either working or trying to sleep. Regardless of my attitude, all was well as we drove back to the boat and cracked into a few beers around 2 am. It was great to have company aboard my freezing cold boat, bouncing and rocking under a windy, foreboding fall night.

A few hours later I was awake, rubbing eyes and cupping my hands around a hot mug of coffee. We took one last trip to the grocery for some snacks and beer. In a whirlwind of shopping, stowing and chatting on my cell phone, the dock lines were untied before noon and we were setting sail in a fading wind and calming sea. Just what I needed, a little time to relax in the company of my brother. After a beautiful sunset, festive dinner and many beers, the winds came up and took us to Gloucester in 24 hours without much trouble and plenty of sleep for the captain and crew.

That night I came to a realization that would help carry me through the next few months. On watch while Adam slept down below, I was lost in the final prep that I would need to do in Gloucester as well as the weight of the adventure at my doorstep. Almost in a full panic, I pledged not to consider the whole trip ever again. I would take on each ocean one by one. Still a big picture, but a calm fell over me in an instant. This intentionally short-sighted thinking would not only continue but progress into a control over my thoughts that I had never before found in my life.

Chapter 6
The Departure

September 30th, 2017
Gloucester Massachusetts

Under a warm sun and calm winds, Adam and I motor sailed past Thatcher's Island and started our approach to Gloucester Harbor. Within a mile or two of the break wall we spotted our Uncle Bill. Bill was the Gloucester HQ so to speak. More excited by the trip than almost anyone, Bill was instrumental in making sure that anything that needed to be done to get me on my way, was done quickly and in style. His love of sailing and pride in Gloucester were infectious and just what I needed over the next 3 days.

With a favorable forecast for the first week of sailing and nothing notable developing between Africa and the Caribbean, the departure date was set for October 3rd. A flurry activity went on in the days leading up to actually setting sail. Sparrow rocked on her mooring and trip after trip was taken from the shore to the boat. Bags of goods, extra supplies, and tools went onto the boat and nothing ever came ashore. A fuel leak developed and the new mainsail needed to be adjusted. The leak was fixed without much trouble but the sail repair had to be left to an expert.

The mainsail is connected to the mast with steel slides every few feet that are fed onto a track. They were the wrong size and needed to be replaced. With only 36 hours until departure, I called my brother Sven about the problem. Having been a sailmaker for 20 years, Sven had a contact in Gloucester and called in a favor. My Uncle Bill and I raced over after dinner with the mainsail and one slide of the correct size. After a few minutes of waiting outside a dark apartment complex, we were greeted by a very happy, very intoxicated sail maker! We went over the problem a few times before I felt that everyone was on the same page and the repair would be done correctly. After many thanks from me and warnings from him about the Southern Ocean, we parted ways. As we drove away, Bill broke the silence with a laugh and said, "that was interesting!" When the sail came back the next day, it was perfect.

Amongst all of the little issues that were taken care of only two major oversights occurred. The first was to acquire some form of antibiotics for me to take on the trip. With all of the other problems that seemed to spring forth, making time to go to a doctor just slipped my mind. I would have to make do with a normal first aid kit, two bottles of aspirin, cortisone cream and an expired bottle of strong pain killers I came across months earlier. The other oversight was my backup computer for downloading weather through a satellite phone. I had left this to Adam, by all accounts a computer genius, but no matter what he tried the sat phone and computer were not compatible. Even the manufacturers of the phone said there was no way to make the two work together. With no time left, I took the computer anyway and would rely on the one I had owned for the last few years as the backup. It worked well and would only be used for downloading weather, otherwise living in a watertight case, safe and sound.

A small group of family and friends had made their way to Gloucester to see me off. I remember Bill laughing as I took video of him cooking blueberry pancakes on the porch of the Gloucester house. I knew this would be something that I would watch over and over while alone at sea. Little did I know this would be a good prod in the backside to get back to that porch and, even more importantly, to get some more of those pancakes!

Glancing constantly at my watch, I wanted to pass the break wall at Eastern Point Yacht Club as close to noon as possible. I am not sure if I was waiting for someone to tell me to leave, but just after 11 am I stood up and announced that it was time to go. Apparently, everyone was waiting for me to make the call. I can only imagine how long we all would have waited there had I not said anything.

Hugs and well wishes abounded as some friends went off to the break wall to watch and the rest came onto Bill's Whaler to drop me on Mighty Sparrow. A few sailed with me the ½ mile to the break wall and emotions were definitely coming to a peak when I needed everyone off the boat before I started breaking down. Another round of hugs, and after being told to "make good choices" I was alone and heading to the break wall. As I passed by, the report of my signal canon came and went with goosebumps forming on my arms. The winds were light from the South, three sails flying, and the first line of information was written in the Ships Log.

As friends and family turned back and faded away, like a flash, the past 4 years flew through my mind. All the work on Sparrow, the money spent, the days and nights practicing for the voyage. I made it a point that this would be the only time I would dive into the past. This trip would have nothing to do with the past but everything to do with the present. The Appalachian Trail allowed me all the time in the world to dissect my life, a good bit of self-therapy for me at the time. Not this trip. It would take practice, but I promised myself to live in the present, dabble in the future, but never go back to the past. I didn't want to miss a single moment of this adventure.

My cell phone snapped me out of setting my mental rules, a quick good luck message from a friend and I started to fire off calls to everyone I had a number for, uncles and aunts, cousins and friends. For the next hour, until the signal ran out, I said good bye to as many people as I could. Maybe I wanted to hold onto the land for a bit longer or just felt like talking to people while I still could. Either way, when the phone went dead, I looked back to Gloucester, but Gloucester was gone. It was clouded in a haze and I was out at sea, alone with Mighty Sparrow, the self-steering wind vane named Mongo, the sea and the sky. The adventure had officially begun.

Chapter 7
Ships Log

1200 March 30th, 2018
Lat 50 24'S, Long 090 46'W
Miles from Cape Horn: 985
Days at Sea: 180

Woke to the inevitable sound of the mainsail slamming! No, no, no! The forecast says I should have wind all day, I was really hoping to avoid the calm after the storm this time. All I can do now is add more sail and hope what little wind I have keeps us moving. I shake out the 3rd and 2nd reef in the mainsail and pole out the staysail. We are moving but with the occasional slam of sails. This always brings worry to my mind as I wonder just how much of this Sparrow can take. In some ways I think the calms are harder for her than the gales.

Regardless of the violent motion I got through my daily checks on deck and everything seems to have made it through the heavy weather without issue. The sewing machine came out and with some blood, sweat, and tears the dodger is fixed and back in place. Not the best job I have ever done but in these conditions, it will have to do. I just wanted my little safety cover back. I am not sure why but I felt 100 times more exposed without the canvas dodger to hide behind from the wind and spray. I think it is just a mental illusion of safety as any big breaking wave could take the thing out again just as it had already done.

I gave the engine a good spray with WD-40, I wish I could do more but I have no extra fresh water and have no dry rags to do any real cleaning. It will just have to wait until I get North and into better weather. It has been over two weeks since I was able to run the engine on account of the motion of the boat and the cold, she really hates to start when the temperature is below 60 degrees. Hopefully I will get a chance in the next few days.

Mongo is doing well but seems to be getting jammed up when I try to change the angle of the wind blade. I figure it must be the buildup of salt and oil in the clicker but I can't waste the fresh water on a good rinse. I am starting to use the oil from the sewing machine now as it is not as thick and will hopefully not build up so much.

Winds increased with a small squall in the night that sent me back on deck to adjust the sails but it soon passed and I was able to get a few hours of sleep. These days the transition from a damp bunk to wet weather gear is not so bad, I just go from wet to wet! If it gets really bad, I will cross the line into sleeping in my wet weather gear and just never take it off, funny that almost sounds nice. It's so wet everywhere I feel as though I am living inside a dog's nose.

Chapter 8
Bad Forecast, the 1st Test

The first 24 hours were fantastic. I love sailing well, with the winds building and a good current pushing me out to sea. Once past the dangers of Georges Bank I felt at ease. I was still having to train my mind to put thoughts of the wild Southern Ocean to rest for a while. I had 2 months or more to get Sparrow and myself ready for that. Besides, I had noticed that the pressure was dropping and winds were veering to the West South West. The forecast called for 25-30 knots of wind and the heavily loaded Sparrow was going to get a good test of her systems right out of the gate. The first day's run of 155 miles was encouraging, and the fact that the blow was coming from the West, in line with the Gulf Stream current, were all good signs.

Hunger had not set in yet, and I was eating only two meals a day though I knew that soon enough I would turn into an eating machine. I had a month of regular food to eat before getting into the packaged and dehydrated meals. In so many ways I felt like I was on just another offshore passage, setting sail for the Caribbean, like I had done many times before. I was at ease for now as the sun set on the second day with winds and seas slowly building and Sparrow happily pushing water out of her way. We were heading East with a bone in her teeth.

I awoke around 0200 to the sound and vibration of

Sparrow surfing the occasional wave. A quick look on deck and the winds were building up and some sail needed to come down. The 1st reef in the mainsail and just the staysail forward seemed to be perfect. The boat speed was the same but Sparrow felt much less pressure on her rig. Mongo was doing great keeping us on course and all was well. Two hours later I woke to a tremendous surf and I was back on deck to find a very different world.

The winds had built well above 30 knots but it was the sea that scared me. Large waves adorned by white breakers illuminated under the almost full moon. I headed Sparrow into the wind a bit to get the 2nd reef in the mainsail and realized just how windy my world had become. When sailing with the wind it is easy to take the sting out of a strong breeze, but turn across or into the wind and you get the full force. Bashing into the waves I was soaked in seconds and struggling to get the sail properly reefed. Once back on coarse, things settled down a bit and Sparrow was once again happy, still surfing the waves at over 10 knots but happy all the same.

I sat on deck as the half-light started to fill the sky. The waves looked menacing but as each breaker approached Sparrow's stern, we seemed to just take off and run away like a nautical game of tag. I was soaking wet but the water was surprisingly warm. I had my answer; I was not anywhere close to the Gulf Stream yet but must have been caught in an eddy. That explained the waves becoming so violent so fast. If the eddy was flowing to the west, against the wind, that would build the seas without warning.

Not long into the blow the ping of metal falling onto the fiberglass deck had me scanning over everything to find the source. The reefing hook that was lashed with spectra line to the Gooseneck had chafed through and nearly fallen overboard. A lucky break for me as I lashed it anew with more than one line this time.

After 16 hours the near gale moderated and I could take account of how we did. 160 miles run! A few weak points discovered, but the big news was that the leaks that I thought were a thing of the past were still there. The sea was dripping in a few spots in the forepeak and in the galley from the scupper above. Drying the food stores in the galley and doing nothing about the leaks in the forepeak, which was mostly a sail locker and would be a salty place for the entire trip, I made note in the ships log and pledged to try to fix them at the first opportunity. Off to sleep for a while as the world outside simply calmed around me.

It is an amazing ability the sea has, to go from good to bad, windy to calm, and wavy to flat. Soon after that first blow came upon us it was gone, all gone. The winds dropped to 3 or 4 knots but it was the sea that surprised me. Hour by hour it became completely flat. As Sparrow entered the Gulf Stream the seas turned to oil. With every bit of canvas up and a good 2 knots of current we were still making good miles due East. The daily routine of boat checks and navigation was underway.

Checking over Sparrow every morning was an absolute must. In reality it is a search for problems or potential problems. I have always found that the "snowball effect" is very pronounced when it comes to boats at sea. Maybe because the environment is so harsh or the reality that if the snowball becomes an avalanche, you sink! The small stitching in a sail that is left unattended can turn into a 3-hour project with a sewing machine when a 2-minute patch could have fixed the problem the night before. My four main checks are a close look over everything on deck, a systems check, navigation/weather, and leaks. Luckily all the leaks on Sparrow are above the water line so not an emergency but more an annoyance, as anyone who sails an old boat knows all too well.

When I walk the deck, I look closely at everything. All screws and pins, stays and halyards, fittings and lashings. If I find that I am finished in only 5 minutes, I go over it again. It is far too easy to overlook something that could turn out to be a big problem. I learned my lessons of a thorough morning check on the watersports beach at the Bitter End Yacht Club. The fleet of small boats needed a good check every day. The problems I found were staggering as those little boat took a pounding for 10 months a year in some of the best winds on the planet. In some ways when I would find something that would have led to a dismasting or rudder failure, I kind of felt like the unsung hero. The next person to take that boat would have had a bad ride and all because of a missing ring ding! I get the same feeling aboard Sparrow, everyday a good slow check over the deck was essential.

The systems check takes only a minute or two aboard Sparrow. Under the guidance of sailors past I kept things simple. The less that can break the better. It also makes sailing on a budget possible. All the gadgets and fancy conveniences that are aboard most modern yachts become more of a headache than anything and cost a pretty penny to boot. I just have to run the bilge pump, look at the AIS, refrigerator, and fresh water tanks. Done.

The only problem I ran into at that point was when I tried to download a new weather forecast. I was only 5 days into the trip but with the unexpected blow and now a flat calm, I wanted to see what was going on around me, especially as I was riding the Gulf Stream. With the strong currents and violent storms that are prevalent in the area, it was no place to linger. First download attempt, nothing; over and over, nothing. A common theme in sailing is that what works on land has a tendency to do the opposite once at sea. I really hate having a computer on a boat but being able to get a detailed weather model anywhere on the planet is wonderful. After 4 hours of working the problem and re-installing the software for the Sat phone I found that a firewall updated the day before I left was blocking the connection. Four hours of frustration followed by a tall drink in celebration as my weather forecast system was back online!

The last check would turn almost into a game for me, the leaky boat game. I would find them and make a note in the ships log. When the weather was calm and I could clean the suspected area, I would go around with 4200 sealant and always say, "That should do it!" In this never-ending game I would take my turn, and then hours or days later the sea would take its turn, and to be honest, I lost this game about 90% of the time. With all checks complete the day would be mine, a noon position plot, reading, sleeping and eating. All with a 360-degree view of an empty ocean, my ocean.

Chapter 9
A Calm and Tranquil Sea

Often at sea a great calm will blanket an area before or after a low-pressure system blows through. For about 3 days Sparrow and I were ghosting along on 5 knots of wind on a mill pond. We sailed under the large drifter sail alone as the weight of the mainsail and boom were too much for the meager winds to fill. But with a helpful current we moved well, averaging about 100 miles per day. If the swell had still been around this would not be the case as the rolling motion would have kept the sails from gripping the wind. Happy as ever we sailed to the South East to put a little distance between us and the Gulf Stream. The potential for violent storms in that area was not worth the free ride.

In the calm weather projects are done by day, enjoying the stars and phosphorescent filled the nights. Sometimes the world would become so beautiful I would do my best to describe the view in my journal.

-Oct 8th Journal:

The Sun fell below the horizon with a glow of pink and orange blanketing the inky sea. As the curtain of night closed, the phosphorescent light filled the sea surrounding Sparrow. As if a halo of blue green light was beaming from her hull. With the sea so flat, only the upset little creatures glowing as Sparrow pushes them reveal that we are still moving. An hour later the moon rose and exposed the horizon that was hidden away in the darkness. For a while I had no clue where sea and sky met as I watched the celestial dance unfold from the bow. How beautiful my piece of the world truly is!

These times were a mix of wonder and sadness for me. I was always so grateful to be out there and a witness to some of the most dramatic sunsets and starry nights, but at the same time I wished that someone was there with me. If only to help explain why I go out to sea to those people who think I am crazy. One thing was for sure, when I would see a great sight that can only be witnessed out at sea, I know exactly why I am out there.

Another sight that is always interesting is that of the great cargo ships that plough through the oceans. I had seen plenty since leaving Gloucester. One night while cooking a spaghetti dinner the AIS alarm cried out and a ship 6 miles out was on a direct line to me. Moving at 18 knots those miles disappeared fast. I watched for a bit as we sailed at only 2 knots on the flat sea, and I could see both navigation lights, red and green, heading right for us. With only two miles to go and no radio contact I remembered what I was doing, cooking dinner, and I realized they might be doing the same!

Quick as I could, I was in the engine room and grasping the valves to open the exhaust and seacock to the water intake. With a finger over the start button I paused, said please, and she fired right up. A look back on deck and I just had to choose a direction perpendicular to the ship. I went North and all 900 feet of metal passed by less than 500 feet from our stern. I shut the engine down and resumed my cooking. I wondered what would have happened if I did not have the AIS? Could our two ships have left from opposite sides of an ocean, traveled thousands of miles, somehow always heading right for each other? What were the odds?

Chapter 10
Ships Log

1800 March 31st, 2018
Lat 51 42'S, Long 087 13'W
Miles from Cape Horn: 865
Days at sea: 181

As we are dipping below 50 degrees South, I am reminded of all the old books about the sailors before me making for Cape Horn. They say the real rounding of Cape Horn is from 50 degrees South in the Pacific all the way around and back to 50 degrees in the Atlantic. So even though I will pass the Cape in a day, I am going to be very exposed down here for more than two weeks! Not a pleasant thought at all. I wonder if I am ready for a Cape Horn Storm? Is Sparrow ready? I figure every lone sailor who ever passed this way asks all the same questions.

Winds have held and the pressure is dropping but so is the wind. It's only a matter of time before the motion of the boat overpowers the wind and I will have to drop the mainsail and just roll with the waves. The most miserable of all conditions I have encountered on the voyage by far, nothing can be done, and Mother Nature controls my world.

I keep eyeing my last can of fruit, sliced Peaches! I promise not to eat them until the Horn but I have been so bad about eating all the good stuff that I doubt my ability to do so. I still have a few pouches of chicken stew and some tuna but mostly it is rice, lentils and oatmeal. When I do add to the staples for a meal, I instantly feel better and more importantly I feel warm! It has been a real struggle to stay warm for the last month while rationing food. I would do anything to get my hands on some cookies and chocolate. I probably spend a few hours each day thinking only about the food I don't have; a waste of time but time is something I have an abundance of these days.

Chapter 11
After you Ophelia

The North Atlantic came alive after three days of calm sailing. A stiff wind was building from the North East and we bashed our way through choppy seas. Pushing hard to keep from having to head due South, my world became very uncomfortable. Heeling over at 20 degrees and lurching over the waves for 48 hours is never a good time. The leaks had overcome my last assault on them and were seemingly growing in number. I noted them and would counter attack in good time. I had bigger fish to fry.

Opening a cabinet for an evening cocktail, a one inch long, filthy cockroach jumped out and tried to get away! I pitched him overboard so fast even I couldn't believe it. I had this problem once before in the Caribbean, they crawl aboard using the dock lines. One of the worst stowaways, second only to rats, one can have on an ocean voyage. If they get out of control and start in on the fresh produce that can be big trouble. But I had prepared for this, and had brought along a box of roach motels which I quickly distributed around the cabin. I never saw another bug that night and I chalked it up to just a random roach alone and lost at sea, but I would never have said that out loud!

Many times, I find that troubles at sea come in waves and

besides the rough weather and insects, a third issue came to light when downloading the new weather forecast. Tropical Storm Ophelia was going to cut right across our path and strengthen into a hurricane in the coming days. Not able to get ahead of her and into the South West winds, I did the gentlemanly thing and changed my heading to due South, letting Ophelia safely pass ahead. In doing so, I was setting myself up for a hard go of beating into the wind and seas, not only in the outer edge of the storm but as it turned out the rest of the North Atlantic Ocean.

As the pressure dropped the wind and seas built, I reduced sail more and more to ease the strain on Sparrow. She was doing well with the waves but shipped water over her bow, which found its way down into the cabin. An annoyance more than anything but if unchecked can become an issue to any electronics or wiring that feel the cold drip of salt water. Besides the leaks, I was bringing aboard a good smattering of the sea with every trip from the deck to the cabin. Sparrow is so small that it is hard to find a place for my soaking wet jacket and pants. On the floor at the bottom of the companionway stairs is all I could come up with. The less moving around the cabin the better; as long as I could keep my bunk free of salt, I could handle a little mess everywhere else.

Late on the night of Oct 17th came a loud bang on deck. Awake from a dream and out of my bunk I saw that the mainsheet traveler car had exploded and was hanging on by one bolt! No time for anything, I grabbed some spectra line and lashed the boom from a block to the deck. Soaking wet and pitching in the seas, I only worried about salvaging as much of the traveler car as possible. Once secure, I went in search of the spare, and with a bit of rummaging, I found it. A few tools on deck with me and an hour later, I had the new car on the track and the mainsheet connected.

Before turning back to my bunk, I put a 2nd reef in the mainsail and had a good long think about what had just happened.

-Oct 18th Journal:

    I always ask myself if I am pushing Sparrow too hard. I need to get East but if I beat Sparrow to pieces doing it what is it really worth? I am glad this happened here and not at the Cape of Good Hope but what is my rush? I have to be more cautious from now on, find the balance between speed and punishment. We have a long way to go...-

    Nothing unnerves me like having something break on Sparrow. Whether it was something I did or something I overlooked, everything comes into question. As happy as I was to get things fixed quickly and to have this happen in a manageable sea, there would be an unease aboard for a few days at least. I was lucky to salvage the broken traveler car and replace the broken bolts; a good thing, as it would now become my only spare! In the light of day, I was able to add some spectra as a safety line so if this were to happen again, the mainsail wouldn't get far and I would have a better chance of a quick fix.

    The close call with Ophelia would be the last bit of excitement in the North Atlantic. Having to head South much earlier than planned, I had unexpectedly positioned Sparrow in a place that would rock my world for the next month. The North East Trade Winds came upon us and soon shifted from the East. The result was a prolonged test of endurance for both Sparrow and me. If we were to make it to the South Atlantic, we would have to sail into the wind for the foreseeable future. I wanted to be closer to Africa as we entered the doldrums and to do that the sails were sheeted in, Sparrow heeled, and the waves sprayed us without restraint. When you live in such conditions it wears on you physically and mentally. There is a strange gravitational pull that controls everything. Moving around is hard and more like climbing. Cooking is limited to cold food and a few risky minutes while boiling water for coffee. Sleeping is hard with the noise of wind in the rig and the creaking joints of every piece of wood in the cabin. My father once described Sparrow as sounding like a popcorn maker when in heavy weather and he was right.

    "Find the noise" was a game played often aboard Sparrow

during the weeks of beating to wind on the way to the Equator. Almost asleep and then clink! One or two waves later, again, clink! With a grumble I would get up and claw my way around, listening for the sound. The source of any one noise is hard to isolate on a fiberglass boat, as sounds can be very tricky to track down. But if I were to get some sleep, whatever was making the noise had to be arrested. Sometimes I would search for almost an hour to find one can of beans rolling only 2 inches against a bulkhead. Hard to believe that so much sound can come from a little thing like that but it happens all the time aboard a boat bashing into the seas.

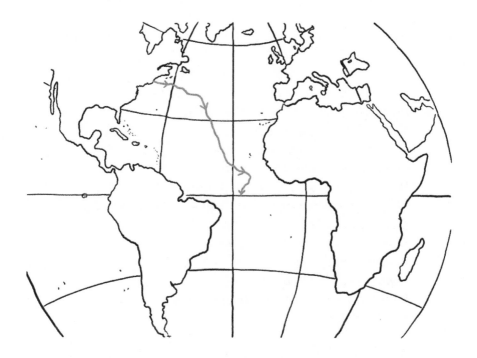

Chapter 12
The Doldrums

Day after day, week after week, we bashed our way South. The winds were relentless, and with only the occasional squall we finally reached the Doldrums around 7 degrees North Latitude. We were just about 300 miles West of where I wanted to be but at least we were making good miles to the South. The tell-tail cumulonimbus clouds were a welcome sight for me.

In this area of unsettled weather under the blazing sun, huge squalls and dead calms prevail. I was still worried about getting further to the East, mostly wanting to avoid another month of beating into the South East Trades once I crossed over into the South Atlantic Ocean. Sailing into the wind and the growing number of leaks were ruling my world and making life quite miserable.

-A poem Oct 27, 2017
These days of sailing against the breeze,
Have taken their toll on little old me.
My bruises hurt and joints are sore,
Nothing is level not even the floor.
Can't set that here or over there
When will it stop, this heeling nightmare?
I lean when I move and lean when I stand, sit or lay.
A level boat? That will be the day!
Alas, it's the ocean I am trying to beat
An unstoppable foe, an impossible feat.
I know I can't win but still I try,
Plying the waves in Mighty Sparrow,
It's do or die!-

By the Beginning of November, the seas had eased up considerably and life became more pleasant. The sea birds hunted flying fish, coasting along with Sparrow as we scared them from the sea and into flight. The birds picked them off or at least tried. I watched one bird try for two hours and never get a bite. It's a tough world out there. I often thought what the life of a flying fish would be like. Constantly attacked from below and above. Always on the run! Even the Mahi Mahi will jump from the water and attack from above. If they didn't have wings, the poor flying fish wouldn't have a chance. And if they are unlucky in the night and find themselves aboard Sparrow, they always ended up in the frying pan.

During this South bound trip in the doldrums, I had one great advantage, the moon. Almost full and very bright, it made spotting squalls easy and erased the worry of being caught with far too much sail up. I tended to stay up late into the night and work the sails in the cooler weather rather than under the blistering sun. The temperatures during the day were a steady

88 degrees above deck and 95 below! Some days were spent in the shade of the Bimini dumping sea water on my head for hours while I read books and listened to music. In the few hours after sunrise and before sunset, I would work on finding the leaks and any other projects that needed attention.

One such problem that was working itself out was my battery system. The biggest power draw aboard Sparrow is the refrigerator. I had 8 pounds of frozen meat that required the coldest setting and most power. In the first part of the voyage, the solar panels were not getting much direct sun and thus I was running the engine more often than I wanted. I needed to get a full charge on the batteries every few days. Now under the tremendous rays of the equatorial sun I had plenty of power but I couldn't seem to get a full charge. The batteries were only 2 years old but had been grossly undercharged for the first year of their life aboard Sparrow. Day by day, with the powerful sun, the batteries seemed to be repairing themselves and holding a better charge.

Nevertheless, I kept Sparrow as simple as I could and would only be running a few fans, the AIS, and the Nav lights. Even a single half dead battery could keep up with that. I had also planned for the possibility of a total electrical failure. I had a few solar lights that could be hauled aloft at night and a backup power pack with a small solar panel and inverter. This would still allow me to charge the computer and sat phone for weather and the Garmin Inreach for position reports to my Mother, Irma. Navigation would just continue with the sextant only but without the comfort of a cross check against the GPS. By this time, though, I was getting very consistent with my daily sights.

As the days passed and we worked our way East, the doldrums awoke with a startling squall that kept me at the helm for two hours. Becalmed and working on securing the gooseneck to the mast track, a very large bank of cumulonimbus clouds approached from the west. Not moving too fast but looking very ominous under the moon light. I quickly wrapped up what I was doing and set the 3rd reef in the mainsail. I then engaged the hydro blade on Mongo, or at least I thought I had.

Within a minute of the moon disappearing and a steep temperature drop, the wind hit. From 0 to 45 knots like a light switch. A once quiet night was filled with the shriek of wind on the rig. Sparrow heeled over and I directed Mongo to fall off the wind, but nothing happened. A look at Mongo with a headlamp and the hydro blade was horizontal and doing nothing. It wasn't broken, it just hadn't been locked into place. No time to go below and get my foul weather gear on, I sat at the helm in boxer shorts. The rain felt like a thousand BB's on my skin and I couldn't face the wind. In the pitch black, head down and feeling Sparrow as best I could, I stole glances at the compass to keep us heading south. To engage the hydro blade on Mongo, I had to hang over the boomkin which I would never want to attempt in these conditions. The waves had been whipped up to a steep chop by the winds and Sparrow bounced violently.

After two hours the winds started to ease and shivering uncontrollably, I crash tacked and Hove-to, bringing Sparrow to a stop and allowing me to get Mongo back online. But first a nip down below to get my wet weather gear on. I came back on deck quite mad at myself and did the job with many disparaging words directed inward. Thirty seconds later, Mongo was sailing as if nothing had happened. Five minutes after that, the wind died completely and all sail was brought down again. The waves still kicking, we rolled heavily and I had a triple share of cocktails under the moon light. Soon I was laughing at the whole situation but taking a good lesson from it as well. I pledged that anything I did out at sea would not only be done right but checked twice!

The following 3 days and nights were almost perfectly repeated. The days spent working with the light changing winds and one monster squall around midnight that would last an hour or two. If anything, it was the most consistent weather I had ever seen in the Doldrums. After the biggest of the four squalls, I came on deck in the half light of morning and became aware of something aboard Sparrow. A large bird trying to balance atop the boom. Wings extended, I tried to only peek at our guest so as not to scare it off, and to my surprise it was an owl! About eighteen inches tall and with a small bird hanging from its beak.

Quick to get the camera because no one would believe this, I took some shots and then watched as she flew away after spotting me. She stayed close for a while as we were all of about 500 miles from the coast of Africa. I can only think that she was taken out in a storm and was looking for a little rest. Also, a place to have breakfast, as I found the remains of another small bird on the foredeck (actually I smelled it before I saw it). What a mess! Feathers everywhere and a full owl pellet! At least she had the courtesy not to relieve herself on Sparrow as well!

While putting a reef in the mainsail during yet another squall, one of the two winches attached to the boom broke free and almost made its way overboard. I shipped the line to another winch on the mast and was staggered when I inspected the empty holes in the boom. Corrosion was everywhere! What also shocked me was that there was no backing plate to truly secure the winch. It had just been threaded into the aluminum boom. I was amazed that the winch stayed in place for as long as it had. Nothing could be done that day with the choppy seas but luckily when I compared the length of my arm from the end of the boom to where the winch once sat, I could just reach it and therefore would be able to carry out the repair.

I had brought aboard some spare wood and even an old wind blade from Mongo. This was very thin ply wood I had covered with a single layer of fiberglass. After drilling the holes and finding the right size bolts, nuts and washers, I could only wait until the seas calmed a bit. As much as I wanted to fix the problem right then and there, at sea, you are at the whim of Mother Nature. I might have been able to remove the boom and go about the repair but the threat of losing a tool over the side or possibly even hurting myself was too great at the time. I could only work on being as patient as I could and checking over Sparrow for any other weak points.

I believe that light winds and calms can be harder on a boat than a gale. The slating of the mainsail stresses the mast and boom. Sails going up and down chafe the halyards. I was seeing plenty of this aboard Sparrow after so many days in the Doldrums. Reattaching the mainsail slides had become a daily routine. This would soon come to an end as I had almost replaced each one with spectra line that wouldn't chafe through. The halyards were puzzling me a bit. I had three that went to the mast head: Main, jib, and a spare. For whatever reason, the lines would jump the shives, cross, and then cut into each other while working the sails. I had lost 6 feet from the main halyard so far and decided to remove the spare that sat in the middle shive. I figured that this would, if anything, give the others a little space. Only time would tell.

Chapter 13
Ships Log

0800 April 1st, 2018
Lat 52 10'S, Long 086 59'W
Miles from Cape Horn: 737
Days at Sea: 182

What a horrible day by all accounts, these are the mental stages I go through when the wind dies completely.
1 Denial-this won't last, the wind will come back and I will just wait, sails up.
2 Frustration-screw it, sails down I am not going to do anything.
3 Boredom-how long can I just sit here steaming mad?
4 Productive-boat check and I work on projects.
5 Positivity-winds are coming back, sails up but slamming hard.
6 Disappointment-slamming too much, sails down, what a waste of energy that was.
7 Happiness-winds fill in, sails up and we are sailing!
8 Forgetfulness-that wasn't so bad, now was it?
Every single time! I go through the same stages like clockwork. But these calms in the Southern Ocean are so different

than in the mid latitudes. Calm is really the wrong word altogether; the wind is calm but the sea is a different story. Even when the waves are only 10 feet, without the wind pressing the sails the boat rolls 30 degrees or more to either side. On deck I watch the masthead swing wildly back and forth, I can't sit or stand without holding on tight with both hands. Below deck the noise of stores shifting back and forth is maddening. I try my best to stow everything tightly but every few minutes something breaks free and cries out as it rolls or bangs from one side to the other. Sometimes I can get some sleep but mostly I just lie in my bunk and listen and wait and hope for the winds to fill back in. It is a sad time for me and morale drops very low. Especially here, so close to the Horn, a place no sailor should ever linger, like parking on the side of a busy highway, it's only a matter of time before you get hit.

Chapter 14
The Ceremony

I had decided before I left Gloucester that I wanted to do something special for the big moments on the trip. The 5 Southern Capes, Equator, Prime Meridian, International Date Line, and Point Nemo. Though only points on a chart while planning the Passage, at sea they mean everything. Mostly they meant progress, something to look forward to and once passed, reflected on. A simple salute to the gods of the sea for letting us pass and a tribute to the next leg of the trip.

It all begins with the hoisting of the flags. The University of Michigan flag atop, CMYC, BEYC, and EPYC below. These flags all have great meaning to me and to my sailing life. I learned to sail working as an instructor at the University of Michigan Family Camp, Michigania. While there I would become an adamant U of M fan, arguably the greatest University in the world. The three Yacht Clubs that would fly all played rolls in getting me to the start line of this voyage. Working at Camp Michigania Yacht Club was the beginning of my sailing career. The money that paid for the trip was earned while working at the Bitter End Yacht Club, and Eastern Point Yacht Club marks the start and finish line.

Once under the flags a splash of rum over the side of Sparrow, careful to touch the hull and run into the sea thus satisfying both Neptune and Sparrow in one go. The next would be a long swig for me! In a way I was not alone during the ceremony. I also had the ashes of Buzz Jenks aboard. The Father of my best friend from childhood, Buzz was more excited about this adventure than almost anyone. He passed away two years before I left. I sadly missed the funeral but was given the highest honor of scattering some of his ashes around the world. So, a bit of Buzz goes from my hand to the sea followed by a splash of rum and another swig for me.

So it went at 0200 on November 10th, 2017. The latitude switched from North to South, and I was free of the squalls and calms as Sparrow pounded South. Still beating to wind, but the new forecast was showing the winds backing to the East. Soon we would be able to reach across the winds and get some miles behind us. For me, the Doldrums are a rollercoaster of weather and emotion. I found myself in awe of the beauty around me and then beaten down by ferocious squalls. I never felt unsafe but always uneasy, looking around like I was walking alone down a dark alley. Instead of shady characters I watched for lightning and angry squalls on the horizon. We had made it through and completed our first ocean crossing of the trip. The North Atlantic would be a memory for the next 6 months, and a fond one at that. Into the South Atlantic we went, 180 degrees on the compass, in-route to the Cape of Good Hope and the wild Southern Ocean.

Chapter 15
South Atlantic Slog

The first few days of my new ocean were very disappointing and uncomfortable. The forecast changed and the beating continued. I wasn't too worried about my heading as it would put me some 400 miles from the coast of Brazil and in safe waters. The threat of pirates nearer the coast is still very real and the more sea room the better. I also wanted to try and sight the Island of Trindade. If all went well, I would be in the area in the next two weeks. It was the sea itself that was getting to me.

Anywhere great oceans meet so do the currents. The Equatorial Current, Guiana Current and South Sub-Tropical Current all play havoc with the surface of the sea. To add to the confusion, the constant squalls would kick up the winds and waves and then leave us bobbing around with no wind for hours at a time. This is frustrating beyond belief. Just when I would think the trade winds were filling in, we would be covered by a cloud that seemed to only want to take the wind from our sails. My only response to this was to drink.

Mighty Sparrow has never been a "dry" boat. I don't see the point in banning alcohol on a boat at sea like so many seem to do. I can understand why one should never be intoxicated at sea, as the potential for making big mistakes is far too great to get sloppy. But nothing is more enjoyable than one or two cocktails at sunset or under a full moon. At this point in my voyage I was just trying to keep my head together and looking for anything that would help me do that. So, if the winds would quit, I would have a drink and then another and so on. If the winds came back, we were on our way and all was well. If they didn't, I would take a nap helped greatly by my indulgence and hopefully wake to the sound of the wind filling in. I would put a considerable dent in my supply of booze over the next few weeks.

November 14th was the day of my only brunch aboard the Sparrow. I was down to the last of the bacon and eggs. A full feast was delayed until I was so hungry, I almost started feeling sea sick. A double helping of bacon was cooked and three eggs scrambled, not by choice but rather Sparrow's motion. Hash browns fried in bacon grease and a good amount of cheese. All wrapped up in two tortillas toasted to a golden brown. People who know me well have often been served up a "breakfast buddy" by yours truly. This would eclipse all that came before. The monster took longer to cool down than it did to eat!

Undeniably the best breakfast I would have for many months to come, I was left with a strong feeling of sadness. Sad to be alone out there and sad to have no more bacon to cheer me up. I remember talking to myself about how much longer I could have had bacon if I was a little more disciplined. It went something like this; "Now you see what you have done? No more bacon for 6 months at least, hope it was good. See all this other food that is so good? Are you going to only eat the good stuff? Or can you control yourself and moderate between boring food and delicious treats? The choice is yours my friend!" I had had many conversations with myself by this point and decided that it was perfectly normal to talk to myself after so many days alone. In fact, it became so normal that if I hadn't spoken a word by noon, involuntarily I would mutter, "pretty quiet today, huh?"

The beating of headwinds and confused seas lasted a few

more days and finally, to my extreme happiness, the winds backed to the East and I was able to head South on a beam reach; the fastest point of sail for Sparrow and much more comfortable. In a few days I would be passing by Trindade and heading further South. I had sailed the South Atlantic from Cape Town to the Caribbean once before but for the first time in many years I was sailing in untouched waters.

One of the biggest components of my diet would be MRE's, basically canned food in a pouch. One such choice I had made was to order thirty Rib Shaped Pork Paddies. I had my first of these for lunch on the 15th of November and within 30 minutes was doubled over on the cabin floor trying to evacuate the gases bubbling audibly from my gut! After a long stint in the head, I was free of stomach pain and vowed only to use the rest of the RSPP's as my last resort to hunger. These 29 useless, disgusting food packets, would come back to haunt me in the coming months.

Clink, Clink, Clink. A new development aboard Sparrow was adding worry and annoyance on a different level at this point. I began hearing a clink every so often coming from somewhere in the mast. If there is one thing that a sailor worries about it is the mast, the power source for forward motion. If something goes wrong up there it can lead to big trouble. So, when I started hearing what I would refer to as "Colonel Clink" I was worried. The sound was most audible when beating to windward and when rolling in a calm. Basically, anytime the mast was swinging from side to side or fore and aft. I thought many times that I had sorted out the problem but eventually I would hear the call of Colonel Clink. And as things do on boats, it was getting louder either from my own attention to it or my imagination.

A change from my normal day came on November 19th when I would see my first bit of land, the Island of Trindade, some 600 miles to the East of Brazil. I would only get within 10 miles of the island but what a sight. After so many days at sea with nothing but the waves and sky, this tiny, rocky island was a welcome sight. I passed to the West of the island opposite the small military settlement Brazil keeps stationed there. The rumors of Captain Kidd's treasure being buried ashore made me want to stop in for a quick look but as usual, I need to keep pressing South.

Almost as fast as the island came into view, it disappeared into a blanket of rain clouds and I never sighted it again. I often wonder what life would be like on one of those isolated islands. I would hopefully be passing by a few more on my way around the world, laying my eyes on places that so few ever have the chance to see. What a privilege, but one that must be earned with days and nights of sailing to get there. Seeing this little outcrop of land stirred so many emotions and thoughts in my mind. What an incredible feeling it is to spot land from the sea. Truly something that can only be experienced to really know just how amazing it feels.

After such an eventful day, sighting Trindade and passing the 20 degrees South latitude, I was getting into an area of high pressure and hopefully light winds. My plan was to get at least one or two days of calm before sailing too far South and into the heavy weather of the "roaring forties." In the calms I wanted to do a very thorough check of the mast, and carry out the growing list of projects that beating to windward caused over the last month.

On November 26th I was able to climb to the top of the mast, still swinging, but in a gentle way, from side to side. I never like climbing the mast at sea. Seems like a sure-fire way to hurt oneself. Even though Sparrow has steps to climb, being aloft always unnerves me. Not even to the top of the mast and I found that the Staysail Halyard had jumped the shive and bent the aluminum plate that holds the block together. I couldn't believe a nylon line could have done that but the pressures that can be created by the power of a winch are incredible. Either way it would have to be replaced and so back down and then back up the mast I went, this time with tools in my pockets.

For small jobs that require only a wrench or screw driver, I free climb the mast. The time and effort it took to rig the bosuns chair are just not worth it. Unless I need to use a power tool or will need both hands for a good bit of time, I will just climb untethered. Though I had been warned against free climbing, I have always found that you pay much more attention to what you are doing, and what Sparrow is doing, when you have to cling on for your life. You become connected to the mast and to the job at hand. Safety is not in the harness but in the forethought, planning and awareness.

After the staysail block was replaced with a much bigger one, I climbed the last ten feet to get to the masthead. What a view! Sparrow is only 32 feet long but from 45 feet above she seems half that size. The sun beat down on my face and the world around me had expanded tenfold from what I see from the deck. Not that anything in my view had changed; it all just seemed far more vast. I wondered what the view was like for the lone sailor atop a 100-foot mast searching for the telltale spout of a sperm whale. They would spend two hours aloft; I was finished with my checks and day dreaming in just over 1 minute! Back down on deck, but this time with the feeling that the mast was stronger. I always felt that way after an inspection.

The latest forecast had given me a glimpse into the world I would soon be entering. 500 miles South of our position, a large low-pressure system was rolling to the East and heading for the Cape of Good Hope. Though I could only see the Northern edge of the system, the winds predicted were up to 60 knots! Far different from the 10 knots of breeze I was sailing in at the time. I wondered if my brother Adam was seeing this as well. He and I had not had to discuss the weather much at all so far. Outside of Ophelia, the winds had been light and variable for the first 6,000 miles of the voyage. No longer able to push the worries of the Southern Ocean to the back of my mind, I now had to prepare for them. Any boat checks were done with more care and if a problem was found it was fixed then and there. Within a week I would be setting a course for the first of the Five Southern Capes.

Chapter 16
Ships Log

1200 April 2nd, 2018
Lat 52 57'S, Long 084 51'W
Miles from Cape Horn: 679
Days at Sea: 183

I managed a little sleep in the light winds but was worried as I had full canvas up, mainsail and light wind drifter, a big problem if a squall hits with that much sail up. I wake up and check the sky's mood often through the night. A small squall came in the morning and the big sails were taken down but I did catch 2 gallons of slightly salty water. I can use it for cooking rice. A check of my fresh water supply shows just under 4 gallons but it looks like more squalls to come, so I could get lucky.

Just plotted our first position on the last unused chart, Drakes Passage! A small-scale chart of Cape Horn so I will plot two or three times a day. It fills me with hope and a good boost for morale to see that the Horn looks so close now but I would never say that out loud. I want to slip by unnoticed. It will be many days after the Horn, before I can even think I am out of danger.

Cold and crisp tonight but the moon has come out and I

spend more time on deck, just staring at the sky. This Southern Ocean has stolen some of my favorite things about sailing; the stars, sun and moon along with any comfort that normal trade wind sailing brings with it. Though I don't dwell on the future, I have thoughts of just how wonderful it will be as we head North into warmer, kinder weather.

Moving well now with just the 1st reef in the mainsail, small squalls rolling through every hour or so and with the sail clean of salt I get a gallon or two from each one! Pure, delicious, fresh water! Things seem to be consistent. The squalls are small, with Sparrow managing them well and rain being collected on its own, so I am off to bed for the night. I feel so much better now that we are moving well and adding to the water, two simple things that make such a difference in my life if only for one day.

Chapter 17
Garbage Everywhere

The sight of floating plastic is normal these days on the open ocean. One or two pieces float by almost every day. A sad truth. I have found some areas of the North Atlantic that seem to be littered with garbage. Often on the trip from the Virgin Islands to Maine, I would see the most garbage just South of Bermuda. What I was seeing by the end of November was the edge of the South Atlantic Garbage Patch. A somewhat disputed area of the South Atlantic Ocean where the currents swirl around and collect large amounts of plastic. For no less than 5 days, the equivalent of almost 500 miles of ocean, I saw garbage all the time. Not piled up like an island, but if I stood on deck and looked 360 degrees around, I would have to count what I saw. Crates, bottles, bags, fishing gear, and styrofoam.

I wished I had a fine net aboard to drag behind Sparrow to see what is just under the surface. I have heard that the broken-down bits of plastic are floating just below. This is the stuff that the fish eat, and that works its way up the food chain to the Mahi Mahi that I would try to catch. Or I should say was trying to catch. I had not wanted to pull out a fish only to find a belly full of plastic. All I could do was feel embarrassed by what I was seeing. There I was, out in the ocean world and it is covered with trash from the land.

Whenever we sailed into an area where I see so much floating trash, the worry of hitting something big creeps into my head. The random container, half submerged and ready to sink whatever boat is unlucky enough to plow right into it. I have never seen one but have heard the stories. I can't keep a watch all the time but I did spend more time on deck during those days. The feeling is much the same as when hiking the Appalachian Trail and thinking about bears. The more you let your mind wander into the horrific stories of bear attacks, the more I would think I was just about to be leapt upon. I figured I had two choices, let my mind wander and thus worry constantly about the slim chance of sailing right into a container, or just put it out of my head and try to forget. Anytime the worry came I would just block it and change the subject.

What snapped me out of my worries on this occasion was, while marking my noon position, the realization that it was Adam's birthday. Thirty-seven years old and how fast time has gone. I had been following my plan to stay in the present while on the trip but figured in this case, I would allow myself an hour or so at sunset to think of the good times that he and I have had over the decades. In his honor, I would drink a few of the beers that I had left and let my mind wander into the past. With all the projects complete and an afternoon of calm winds I put the trash to good use and fired off a few rounds with the shotgun. It was the first time I had targets to aim at and I needed the practice!

By the beginning of December, we were making our way to the East. Still 1,500 miles to the West North West of Cape Town, worries about my dwindling fresh water supply were on my mind. I was trying to remember the last shower I had and the last time I was able to clean down below on Sparrow. Everything was a bit greasy these days. At least it was no longer hot. The cool air kept me from sweating, unlike in the tropics. As for the water supply, it was getting low. About 10 gallons in the main tanks and then 5 more in jugs under my bunk. It just didn't rain in the South Atlantic and even though I had cut back on how much I was using, the current level was becoming a worry. I would have to get out the desalination pump if things didn't change soon. My hope was that as we made our way further South the rains would come.

My first conversation with a ship, Santos Express, was late on December 1st. 1,000 feet long and making 18 knots fully loaded. They were heading around the Cape of Good Hope and wondering just what a small sailboat was doing this far out to sea. We talked about the trip and how to follow my positions. We also talked about the weather. A big system was coming up from the South and going to slam into the Cape in about a week. They would be dealing with that one, but we would still be far away. No doubt having to deal with the next big system, as they tend to roll in every few days or so. With wishes of good luck and following seas, the VHF fell silent and was turned off once again.

It amazes me that in the 18 years that I have been venturing offshore the communication between ships at sea has completely changed. Before AIS it was common place to call any ship that was sighted, and more often than not, you would get a response. Like two workers meeting in the break room for a quick chat before heading back to what they were doing. Now it seems that with the information provided by AIS, mostly the knowledge that two ships are not on a collision course, there is no need to communicate. A great tradition that has sadly been lost at sea. After so many attempts to hail ships without response, I still turn on the VHF and just hope that they might be curious about my intentions. What I didn't consider was just how empty the Southern Ocean truly is. In the Atlantic, we cut across shipping lanes regularly but the Santos Express was the last ship I would see for the next two months.

The weather was beginning to show me just what I was in for. Softly at first, but with all the traits of a Southern Ocean low-pressure system. The wind freshened to F-6 from the North West and then abruptly changed to the West and then South West, building up the seas from three directions. In this first blow the winds never exceeded F-7 but plenty of sail changes and even a jibe was required to get through. Within a day, we were totally becalmed in a confused sea. The main sail was slating so hard that it eventually had to come down and thus the rolling became much worse. Morning cocktails led to a good bit of sleep and when I awoke, it was to the sound of waves lapping against Sparrows hull. The winds had filled in from the South and the sails were set like so many times before, but something was different.

For over a month with the winds blowing generally from the East, we sailed on a Port Tack. One gets very used to the heel of a boat. You dump food scraps and coffee grounds over the low side and after a month this becomes a mechanical motion. We had now begun sailing on the Starboard Tack and were heeling to the opposite side. My first attempt to toss coffee grounds as I had for so many weeks, ended in the cockpit being covered! On the new tack the world felt like it was upside-down! A welcome change for sure as sleeping is better aboard Sparrow on this tack with no need for the lee cloth. I was able to wedge myself against the side of Sparrow now. Cooking was far safer as the stove was below where I would stand. If a boiling pot of water, for example, decided to become mobile it falls away from me instead of on top. The only drawback was the Nav station. Before I would recline in my chair and make out my position. Now I had to wedge myself in using both feet and one arm. The ships log and my journal would suffer from poor penmanship on a Starboard tack.

My new world faded away after just two days as the winds came back from the North and became steady at F-5. In five days, Sparrow had sailed better than ever before with daily runs of 155, 150, 144, 144, 176! If only the wind and sea would stay like this I thought! I would be around the world in no time. But then anyone could do it and what would be the point of that. I spent this time in good wind to fine tune Mongo and make sure he was not having to work too hard. The hydro rudder swings from side to side, 24 hours a day, every day. What I didn't want to see was the rudder swinging until it would bottom out. In normal conditions the pressures were easily managed by Mongo but soon we would be surfing waves and then the pressure would really test everything. I had an old Aries Wind vane break one of its supports and almost detach completely from Sparrow during a sea-trial. The result of a massive amount of corrosion coupled with the hydro rudder slamming from side to side while surfing waves. I was able to save the Aries that time but wanted to avoid having to deal with such a situation again.

What I found after so many miles under the helm of Mongo was that, if Sparrow was balanced well with the sails, Mongo was happy. When we were overpowered, Mongo could be adjusted to counter the force and again was happy. But when overpowered and surfing, Mongo was working far too hard and couldn't keep the hydro rudder from hitting each side support. The solution was simple; reduce sail. Mongo had been taking care of me so far and I needed to return the favor. I didn't even want to think about having to hand steer for hours and days on end.

On December 5th the Flags went up on a beautiful day. Just before noon we had passed the Prime Meridian! Drinks all around! Buzz, have a good one! Cheers to you! I let the flags fly for a while this time. They still looked so crisp and new, they no longer fit in with the worn look of Sparrow and me. We were becoming ragged and weathered just as one should after so much time at sea. As I looked upon each of the flags, I wondered how many people had found out about the trip and were following our progress. I can only think that word must be spreading by now. I was hesitant to advertise my voyage as the chances of success are so low. So many have tried and failed. If that were to happen to me then the fewer people that knew, the better!

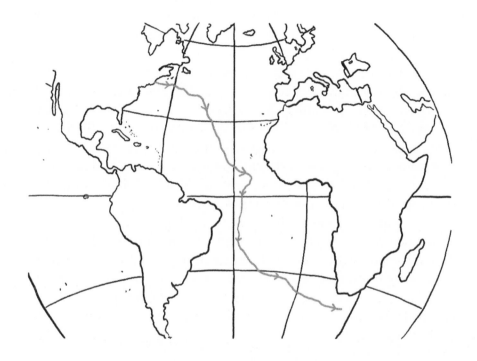

Chapter 18
Cape of Good Hope

On December 8th the winds had increased to F-7 from the South. I was in the trailing edge of a system heading for the Cape of Good Hope. The pressure was rising and my only thoughts were to get East as fast as we could. We had finally reached 40 degrees South latitude but still had some 600 miles until the longitude of Cape Town and then another 500 miles or so to be clear of the Cape. During the blow, we were down to our 3rd

Reef in the mainsail with the staysail flying as we power reached along. Soon the winds backed to the South South East and the ride became much more uncomfortable. Having to stay on a heading of due East meant beating to wind and bashing into the seas. The forecast had the winds dropping fast so we pushed hard while we could.

What followed this first blow was a calm that lasted 48 hours. During that time we only made 87 miles and spent many hours rolling in an endless South West swell with little to no sails up. With every puff of breeze, the sails went up then usually right back down after only a few minutes, 12 times in one day! The night of December 10th was spent just drifting and listening to the songs of whales through Sparrow's hull. A spooky night for sure, alone and listening to the ghosts of the deep.

Unable to sleep well I went on deck for a late-night inspection and found the outhaul line had jumped its shive at the end of the boom and needed to be fixed immediately. Anything to take my mind away from the monsters of the deep. So, under the light of a headlamp, tools came out and the project was completed in an hour. I would have to keep the tension on the outhaul from now on, to prevent it from happening again. After the fix, I enjoyed the phosphorescent animals that danced all over the sea. I must be within the reach of the Agulhas Current. Sea life abounds in areas where currents collide. It is also a place where bad weather can become horrific.

An update from Adam on the position of the Agulhas Current told me that I needed to get further South. Down another degree at least to 41 degrees South latitude. The pressure had begun a steady drop and by noon on December 12th it was down to 1006. Winds filled in from the West South West and it seems that this next system was doing the same as the one before. The Gale was coming up from the South and catching me in its trailing edge. The only difference was the size and intensity.; a much larger storm, and forecast to develop hurricane force winds in the coming days. Luck was on my side, as the system would be well to the East by then. If I had not been becalmed for those two days, I would have surely gotten a good beating.

As the winds steadily increased throughout the day, I did what all sailors do as heavy weather approaches. Check systems and get the boat ready. This would be the first Southern Ocean Gale and my plan was to run under the staysail alone. By sunset the winds had increased to F-8 and under just that one sail we were still moving fast. The mainsail was lashed to the boom and a second sheet had been made to the staysail leading out to the tracks for the Jib. The purpose of this was to have a secondary line in case the other lets go, and also to be able to adjust the sheeting angle if needed. I really didn't have any idea what would work best. To be honest I was scared and just needed to think I had options if trouble arose.

The storm jib was brought out from the forepeak for easy access, as well as the 300-foot line for towing astern if the surfing got out of control. By midnight the pressure was down to 993, winds from the South West at F-8 or more, temperature was 60 degrees, and squalls rolled around us. The building seas were still only about 15 feet as an average but every so often a big set would come in and I could feel Sparrow lifting much more than before. I was getting very tired after the day of anticipation but wanted to stay ready. Instead of getting out of my wet weather gear I chose to move a few cushions onto the cabin sole and try to sleep there, fully clothed and ready to get on deck quickly if needed.

I think it is worth noting that most of the planning in storm tactics that I was ready to employ were coming from the books written almost 50 years ago. I figured that they were the most appropriate for my voyage as Sparrow and her equipment were very much the same as what was being used at the time of the Golden Globe Race in 1968-69. I wanted to have as many options as possible. If the conditions became too much for one method, I could switch to the next and so on. For this gale, we would ride under the staysail alone and if the surfing became uncontrolled from the increasing winds, I could change the staysail to the storm jib to slow the boat. If the seas became too large and breaking, I would try towing my line with an anchor attached to slow Sparrow down. The one tactic I didn't plan to use was lashing the tiller and going below to take my chances. Lying a Hull and going Hove-to would be the absolute last resort. The idea of just letting Sparrow get pounded sounded crazy to me. I wanted to be a moving target if anything. Plus, I wanted to get the hell out of the Southern Ocean as fast as possible and to do that, we needed to hold on and go for a ride!

At first light I had taken a look on deck and was shocked at the size of the swell that had built up in the night. Like rolling hill sides, I could have fit a stadium between them. When Sparrow was lifted to the top, I could see for miles astern, just more watery hills marching endlessly from the South West. In the trough I could only see the next wave coming. I can only guess but the average swell height was around 30-35 feet. Every so often I would see what I referred to as "lumber jacks." The random, extra-large waves that lurk around and, in my mind, threaten to chop my mast down by rolling Sparrow over without a second thought. These are both horrifying and amazing to see. Even over the howling winds I could hear them breaking in the distance, a low rumble. In my head it sounded like someone saying "Hey Sparrow, where are you? I am going to find you!"

With each wave, breaking or not, Sparrow would be lifted up and the wave would pass underneath her hull, the breakers clamoring along her canoe stern unable to grab hold. It was marvelous to see Sparrow so able to handle the seas. The staysail was just perfect in the F-9 winds, with only the occasional bang when the winds let the sail collapse and then fill with a fresh gust. I had thought about using the spinnaker pole to hold the staysail in place but I worried about having to change sails in the middle of the night and dealing with the heavy pole on a pitching deck. I once again figured that simple was going to be better. For the most part, it worked well.

We didn't sail without a few troubles during the gale. With just the staysail I found that I needed to sail approximately 30-40 degrees from dead down wind. A little more than I wanted, but if we went to 20 degrees the jib would collapse and fill violently far too often. The jolt on the rig and the noise were far too unnerving. Sailing at such an angle, the odd wave would push Sparrow's stern and overpower Mongo. If I left Mongo alone to correct our course, it would take over a minute and leave Sparrow's beam exposed to the seas where we would ship plenty of water aboard. And so, I spent plenty of time on deck ready to help Mongo in his fight against the gale.

Down below was a wet mess! Besides the sea that was brought below by the soaking wet crew, the leaks were in full drip. Only my bunk and Nav station were spared. The charts would need a good toasting over the stove when things calmed down and the rest of the cabin was going to need a good wipe down. For now, I could only live with the current conditions of everything being wet. By noon, we had covered 151 miles and the pressure had bottomed out at 990 and began slowly increasing.

At sunset the winds had come around to the South and eased to F-7, so the 3rd reefed mainsail was hauled up slowly. I spent more time hanging on to a very lively Sparrow than raising the sail. Once set, the motion improved considerably. I have always found that a boat overpowered is slow to get me moving to reduce sail, but when she is underpowered it is very obvious. The motion is terrible. Rolling to either side, without making much way, even the sound of water passing by the hull disappears. Throughout the night as the winds eased, more sail went up every hour or so. By noon the next day the winds had quit and we were left in some serious "slop and chop," with no sail flying and making no way at all.

So horrible was the motion, and even though we had just weathered our first real gale, there was little to be happy about. Until that is, I charted the noon position and found that we had passed the Longitude of the Cape of Good Hope! Our first of the 5 Southern Capes! At least I would have something to do; the Ceremony! The flags were hoisted but didn't exactly fly without the wind, though they filled as the mast swung on its 60-degree arc. So happy yet so disgusted by the lack of wind and large seas, I doubled the ration of whiskey, at least for me! One for Sparrow, one for me, one for Neptune, one for me, one for Buzz and one more for me! I can't be sure if it was the high from passing the Cape, weathering the gale, or the whiskey, but I broke into a rousing round of the Victors!

After a good long sleep, the winds began to fill back in and full canvas was flying, full mainsail and large drifter. Just because we had done so well in the last blow, I did not want to experience another. I wanted to get away from such a foreboding place as fast as possible. My goal for the coming week was to put as much distance as possible between us and the Cape of Good Hope. I also intended to get a little further North, as I planned to cross the Indian Ocean between latitude 36-38 degrees South. Funny enough, I had nothing to do with getting my wish in spades.

Ocean currents can be a tremendous hazard when the wind blows against them. Two of the most powerful on the planet are the Gulf Stream, along the East Coast of America, and the Agulhas Current, that flows down the South East Coast of Africa. Both currents look like rivers with the main stream flowing in the center and wild eddies breaking free on both sides. I was sent a list of waypoints from Adam that formed a corridor for the next few days. They ran a little East and then to the North East, no wider than 40 miles. "Stay in the waypoints and go for a ride, strong counter current" was included in the message. As the seas around us calmed and the winds stayed light, Sparrow and I were about to go on a Magic Carpet Ride!

Just before entering Adam's coordinates, the seas were very unsettled. Sailing with full canvas still and in just F-3 winds the sea would heap up and start breaking, then smooth out like glass. Our boat speed was fluctuating from 6 knots to 3 knots. Obviously I had wandered into a convergence zone with the currents. I could only imagine what a F-10 gale would be like in this place. Capable of sinking the most seaworthy of ships.

During the next two days, I figured my boat speed was around 5 knots, the rest was the Magic Carpet. I would see speeds up to 10.3 knots over the ground at times. To experience this on a calm sea and in light wind is a strange feeling. Erie to know you are moving fast but all you see is normal sailing.

Either way, I was happy to have this boost. Full sail and heading North East, just where I wanted to go. The information about the currents was a godsend. However, it wasn't long before things got ugly again.

The winds woke me from a dead sleep around 0300. On deck, Sparrow was pounding into a wave set from the North while almost surfing the swell from the South West. Down came the #3 jib, and before it was packed away and down below, the winds had risen and the 1st reef went into the mainsail. By noon, the wind was at F-8 and the seas were breaking everywhere. The rain pelted me and burned my hands as I lashed the mainsail to the boom. All this was happening very fast. I had been through the squalls in the Doldrums but this was something that carried with it a different weight. Maybe it was the confused seas or just that I was still within the reach of the Cape, but I worried as the winds started to take the tops from the waves. Soon the surface of the sea was white with spray, and in the rain I could only see 100 yards. By 1500 I could only estimate the winds at F-10 when the squalls rolled over us like a white blanket. The mast shook and wind shrieked through the rigging. I remember having to tell myself to stop grinding my teeth as I looked out from the plexiglass hatches and wondered if Sparrow could hold together.

Within a few hours the winds were back down to F-7 and my brain could take a break from the worry. Looking at the forecast, I should have been in 25 knots all day! The pressure only dropped a little then came right back up. I can only think that it was an isolated storm cell, a Southern Ocean Squall. The effect this had on my mind was just adding to the awareness of the dangers that abound this far South. The weather was showing us just how quickly it can go from good to bad.

Chapter 19
Ships Log

0700 April 3rd, 2018
Lat 53 19'S, Long 082 28'W
Miles from Cape Horn: 589
Days at Sea: 184

Woke to the slam of the mainsail again today, I really hate that alarm clock. Winds have fallen below 10 knots and the seas keep the sails from gripping the winds. If only the seas were flat, I could sail, it is very frustrating. A feeble attempt of a few different sail combinations resulted in circling back to the slamming mainsail and slowly moving East.

Strange looking squalls all around. They seem to be more like a cloud bank. A white wall right down to the sea. As the first round rolled over, I realized very quickly, I was now in the realm of snow and hail. Marble size balls of ice shooting like BB's across the sea. I was down below as soon as I could reduce sail. I am keeping my ski goggles within reach at all times from now on.

As the first round passed, I went to work on collecting as much hail as I could. The rain catch was jammed up and the 1st reef in the mainsail was full. I am not sure if the water will be drinkable once melted but maybe I can use it for cooking. Fresh water stores are just below 10 gallons but I have a feeling in the coming days, I will get more chances to scoop more snow and hail.

I have been warming my hands over the stove more and more these days. The cold is getting very hard to deal with. I am not sure why but I just can't seem to shake this cold deep down in my core. The cabin warms with the stove but the second it is off we go back to freezing. My only defense is to wear everything I have including wet weather gear all the time. I am glad I brought my sleeping bag with a 32-degree temperature rating. The bag along with all the layers of thermals is just keeping me from shivering.

The sky is unsettled at best, squalls roll in and sails need changing all day and into the night. I am so tired and so hungry, rice for dinner with one of the last packets of chicken stew. I am so glad I saved a few for the Cape Horn approach. For once my will power held out!

Chapter 20
All the Water in the World

As we slipped past 30 degrees East Longitude and out of the reach of Good Hope, my fresh water supply was becoming dangerously low. Though I had been able to catch a few gallons here and there, I was under 10 gallons and finally brought out the emergency desalination pump. In the calms I could sit on deck and pump away with the hose directly in the sea. If we were moving well, I was forced down below with two 5-gallon jugs, one filled with the sea and the other slowly filling with fresh water. When I say slowly, I think the term glacial is more accurate. One hour of constant pumping would produce just about 1 gallon of water. The only thing I could do to not be discouraged was to think in terms of how many days it would last me on my current ration of 64 ounces per day. 144 oz divided by 64 equals 2.3. Thus, each hour I pumped I was getting another 2 1/2 days of water. Sometimes I would pump for 5 hours a day. That was until the 21st of December, as we sailed about 600 miles East of the African Coast.

A beautiful day by all accounts, I had a nice cocktail of scotch and water. The sun was out, seas were calm and all I had to do was pump. After about 5 hours and 5 gallons of fresh water produced, crack! The sound still echoes in my brain. I knew I had just lost my safety net. The plastic casing had let go and upon inspection, I thought I might be able to fix the problem. But first I needed a dead accurate count of just how much fresh water I had onboard. Split into three different tanks, I figured I had 15 gallons in total along with 6 liters in the life raft. Only in an extreme emergency was I going to open the life raft to find the water. Never a good idea to tamper with a life raft, so I left the supplies out of my calculations. At my current rate, I had about 30 days of water.

My first attempt at a fix was with a two-part epoxy glue that failed miserably. Not even two pumps before the pressure cracked the new seal. The second and third attempts involved more glue, turn buckles, and spare metal plates. All failed. The pressures were just too much to overcome. In the meantime, while waiting for the glue to harden, I had made a better rain catch system; something I could leave lashed to the mast pulpit for quick action. A simple rig that used the mainsail under its 1st reef. The excess sail formed a gutter and any rain that hit the sail would run right into it. A perfect system by all accounts that depended on only one thing, rain. Not only rain, but enough of it to rinse the salty sails for a few minutes and then keep going while the 5-gallon jug fills up.

Morale aboard the Might Sparrow was reaching an all-time low as the holiday season came in. Although just another date in the ships log, it was impossible not to be pulled back to life on land. My mind was constantly wandering to rooms filled with friends and family. Warm fires and a snow-covered world outside of every window. Not to mention the image of them all sitting around a big table and enjoying a delicious meal. I am sure they would be talking about the missing person, out on the ocean, dealing with issues that none of them was aware of. I pictured the water glasses. One per person, flowing freely from a big pitcher sweating from condensation. What I would have given to have a spot at that table! For me, it was Sparrow, the sea, and the sky. Along with a serious shortage of fresh water.

After 4 attempts to fix the water pump, I had to give up and let the new reality flow over me. I had to accept the new challenge. When I had the ability to make fresh water, it was a feeling of independence from Mother Nature. I was in control, no matter how annoyingly slow it was to produce. I could still produce it. Now I could do nothing but watch how much I had and do my best to collect every drop that fell from the sky. If anything, I can say that I was very uneasy with the thought of slowly running out.

The winds came in bursts as we put more and more miles between us and Africa. We sat and rolled in no wind on Christmas Eve, then 30 knots and building seas came up by sunset on Christmas Day. Always watching the wind spin around the compass, first North then West and then South. Churning up the waves each time and making steady sailing a distant memory. The weather systems did have one pattern that I had been noticing. Just as the front line passes and the winds shifted from North to West, rain squalls would accompany the shift. I did what I could to position us in front of the approaching rain. My Christmas gift was 2 gallons of fresh water to add to my supply.

Steady winds came in for three days as we pushed ever Eastward. I would be flying high as the miles added up each day. In the calms I screamed and cursed, and when the winds filled in, I would thank Neptune and try to catch up on sleep. My journal entries read like a record on repeat. Becalmed and in a terrible mood; winds filling in and moving well again; reefing down the sails and holding on; becalmed again and cursing the ocean around me. Sparrow dealt with the ups and downs much better than I did. It seems that each day I would go from the edge of tears to being euphoric in a matter of hours. Over and over, day after day, we pressed on further from land and into the vast stretches of the South Indian Ocean. No matter the trouble I was having both physically and mentally, the goal remained the same, keep moving East!

Chapter 21
Collision Course

The New Year brought with it a message of warning. A tropical depression had formed off the West coast of Australia and was building. The cyclones in the South Indian Ocean can flow to the West and then take a turn to the South and dissolve in the cold waters of the Southern Ocean. These storms rarely make landfall and are of little concern, unless of course one is sailing across the Indian Ocean in January.

My first warning was from Adam. He was keeping an eye on the system as it developed and would let me know if trouble was coming. The forecasts I was downloading were for smaller areas around my position at the time, so I saw nothing but calm winds coming for at least a week. If the seas would just ease up a bit, I could ghost along and continue gaining miles. By January 6th the winds had all but died and only 45 miles fell in our wake. At one point, with no sails up, we slowly drifted .5 knots to the West! My frustration was reaching its pinnacle. The water pump, the calms, and now this Cyclone, I would have given anything to end the trip then and there. Lucky for me, in the middle of an ocean it is impossible to just give up, and the thoughts of quitting gave way as they always did. Amazingly, the seas did ease up, and even though the winds were only ever F-1 or 2, we kept moving slowly East.

Full sails up both day and night under clear skies. And

although only a breath of wind, things seemed to be consistent compared to the weeks of sailing away from the Cape of Good Hope. Reports about the officially named storm, Cyclone Irving, came in with suggestions of how to avoid a collision course. Joining Adam was Mike Porter, a great friend and fellow captain whom I trusted without question. With each new update I would sense a little more concern for my situation in both sets of messages. But it was when my two weather guys had talked to each other that I realized this was going to be a close call.

When trying to position oneself in a hurricane or cyclone there are some tactics involved. With Irving coming down from the North toward my position I had two choices. Turn West and let it pass just as I had with Ophelia, or press on and try to out run it. The winds of Irving were spinning in a clockwise direction angled slightly toward the center. So, on the Western edge of the storm the winds would be coming from the South and on the Eastern side, from the North. What makes one side the "safe side" is the movement of the entire storm. Let's say that Irving was moving at 15 knots to the South and the winds are 70 knots around the center. On the East side of the storm the 15 knots are added to the wind speed as they combined together. On the West side, the 15 knots can be subtracted as the movement of the storm takes away from the wind speed around the center. Thus, a difference of 85 knots to 55 knots, assuredly a very big difference! This is a big-time simplification of how to deal with cyclonic storms at sea, but aboard Sparrow at that time, this was what I was facing. Making a choice between which side I was going to be closest to. With less than a week until we would meet, Irving was the only thing on my mind. That is until the sea turned red.

I had spotted plenty of whales along the way, mostly South of Good Hope. Various types and usually at a good distance. One day, I even saw the very distinctive square head of a sperm whale plowing through the wake of Sparrow. But as I approached the sea mount surrounding St. Paul and Amsterdam Islands, the ocean was taking on a ting of red. Barely discernable at first, I thought maybe it was a red tide or algae bloom. Soon, I was seeing what I can only describe as bright red paint on the water, stretching to the horizon in streaky lines. I finally put a bucket over the side and investigated. What I found were hundreds of ant sized red shrimp. It was Krill. In the bucket I had maybe 1,000 of them, and looking up at the ocean, I realized that I was sailing through them in the trillions! For the first time in my life at sea I fully understood how something so small could feed the largest animals on the planet.

Seeing any life at sea always amazes me. More so, after seeing nothing but birds for weeks. When the ocean comes alive it does so with a bang. I still remember uttering the question aloud, "I wonder where the whales are?" The very next morning, January 9th, started just like so many before. Awake at sunrise, in light wind conditions. Before breakfast, I went on deck to check the world around me. Not one foot out of the cabin and I was greeted by a stinking cloud of spray. To my great surprise, a whale had just surfaced not more than 5 feet from Sparrow! Outpacing us as we were only making about 3 knots of speed, another blast, this time from astern. Two whales that were very interested in Sparrow. At first, they just surfaced and swam around us, as if just coming in for a look. It occurred to me at that point that the color of the anti-fouling bottom paint I put on Sparrow was almost identical to the color of the Krill. Did they think I was a moving cloud of Krill, were they ready to take a bite and see if they found the mother lode?

The stories of boats being sunk by accident or on purpose by whales came flooding into my brain as I watched and filmed with a shaky hand. Sometimes they would flank me on both sides, and other times they disappeared for a few minutes under the surface. After about 30 minutes, one of the two either got very curious, or as I like to think, spotted me looking over the side in amazement and terror. What followed was a spectacle that I will never forget. With all of its 35 feet, this whale would swim within 2 feet of Sparrow along the beam. After spraying us down, as if saying, "take that," it would tilt on its side and come just about to the surface. This gave me the view of its white underbelly, fins; and being so close; barnacles. Sometimes the edge of its tail would be so close to Sparrow's rudder I could have reached out and touched it! Over and over it did the same thing, closer and closer until I was sure we were going to get a bump. This whale, human, boat interaction lasted for over an hour. Acting more like dolphins than whales, I was shocked at how agile these giants truly were.

In the following days, I would see plenty of whales feeding in the distance and blowing their spouts. But nothing with the intensity of that morning. I felt as if I was given a rare gift, one of the many times I wished that someone else was aboard to share the experience. It wasn't until the new weather report came in that I was snapped out of the dream-like encounter with the whales. Things had changed, and not for the better.

The path of Cyclone Irving had changed slightly to head more to the South South East instead of due South. All around us the seas were calm and the winds were light, and we ghosted along to the East, slowly. Adam was recommending that I turn back to the West and let this one pass by, better safe than sorry. Looking back on the situation I can see that he was right. But in the mental state that I was in, frustrated, tired, and moody, the thought of turning around and loosing miles that I had work so hard to put behind me would have been horrible. Each hour we backtracked I was sure I would be in a rage. Not only that, but with the storm track always changing it would still be a bit of a gamble, albeit the safer one as it would most likely keep me on the "safe side" of the storm.

Looking between the weather models, the chart, and the ocean around us, I decided to push forward and take my chances. I also feared for my mind. The emotional rollercoaster that I had been riding meant that my nerves were shot, and to lose what I saw as a week of sailing was going to push me over the edge. An edge that I have been dangling over since entering the Southern Ocean.

January 9th and 10th were almost identical. With very calm conditions, it seemed that Irving was sucking up every bit of wind for hundreds of miles around. The calm before the storm is a very real phenomena in every ocean. The pressure was at 1014 at noon on the 10th; by the next morning it had begun to fall a millibar per hour. By 1800 on the 11th, the winds had reach F-8 and were building the seas up. The edge of Irving was upon us.

Still studying the weather models, we had made enough miles to be well away from the center of Irving and its most powerful winds. As the wind was coming from the North, I set Sparrow up to sail as fast as she could go. We power reached across the wind and seas at more than 6 knots. I was pushing her hard but this was the time to do it. With the occasional breaking wave giving us a good hit, the seas didn't seem to be getting up to the size that would require us to run with them. Also, running with the winds would keep us in the storm for much longer; we wanted out and as fast as possible. So, reaching away we dashed between the waves and all seemed well. The winds held at F-8, and just after midnight I was so exhausted from stress I headed for my bunk.

What followed was completely of my own doing. For hours we had been sailing well and without anything but the odd hit of a breaking wave. All I was thinking about was getting away from the eye of Irving. So, we sailed perpendicular to the storm's path. What I hadn't considered was that as I slept down below, things could change. To this day I don't know if it was a much larger wave than the others or if the seas had just started breaking enough to become dangerous. Either way, around 0300 the impact happened like an unwelcome alarm clock. I can only equate the sound of the wave that hit Sparrow as a high-speed car crash, involving a bus! The kind of thump that you feel when you watch powerful fireworks at a close distance. I also felt Sparrow rotate about 90 degree on her side. My lee cloth had become a hammock that I was now trying to step from to get on deck. No sooner had I reached the companion way hatch before we were back upright, Sparrow's sails luffing loudly for a few seconds and then filling with wind. I couldn't see any damage, but adjusted Mongo to sail off the wind and with the seas. We then flew down waves at great speed for the rest of the night. My night's sleep was over and I went about mopping up the small amount of water that had been brought in through the galley sink, hatches, and every leak Sparrow had!

At first light I could see that one of the stanchions had bent a small amount and the spray skirt had lost a few of the grommets that held it in place. The preventer was broken at the metal clip which secured it to the boom. I never even looked for it when the knockdown happened and we had sailed the rest of the night without one! Down below there was almost nothing out of place, though the forepeak looked as though it had been flipped upside-down. I figured that besides being very lucky, we were hit by a breaking wave just big enough and with sufficient force to knock Sparrow flat. But that was it. The wave had used everything it had in the initial hit and there was nothing left. I say lucky because if the wave had been any bigger, we could have been rolled over and possibly lost the mast. At the same time, we were unlucky that the wave found us in the first place.

Two things I learned from the knockdown. One is that if there is even a thought that being beam to the sea is getting a little risky, then stop doing it. The second was that luck was going to play a big role during the rest of my time in the Southern Ocean. The sea can overwhelm a boat of Sparrow's size without a thought. We could do our best to stay clear of big storms but in reality, we were completely at the whims of Mother Nature. Mentally, I was very disturbed by this point in the voyage. The weather, the water shortage, and the fact that I was about to head deeper into the Southern Ocean were all weighing heavily on my mind. At my current position I was expecting at least another 3 months of these conditions. Sparrow was holding up better than her Skipper. The shift from me sailing Sparrow to Sparrow carrying me was taking place.

Chapter 22
Ships Log

0200 April 4th, 2018
Lat 54 05'S, Long 079 54'W
Miles from Cape Horn: 483
Days at Sea: 185

Winds are building and we are flying through the night! Very nervous for the random squall as the sky is just a black void tonight. Sparrow is holding her own in the shifts and gusts. She allowed me a few hours of very restless sleep but sleep all the same. A quick check on deck and Sparrow, the Mighty Sparrow, not only made it through these squalls and calms without waking me but I found the water jug with over 2 gallons of perfect fresh water! What a gift, what a boat!!! For these last few weeks Sparrow has carried me through. I try to take care of her as my duty but recently it has been the other way around, I am being taken care of.

So far 3 more gallons of fresh water from melted snow! A little victory for sure and I now see not gallons but days, days that I will be able to stay at sea and possibly increase how much I can drink. I won't even mention the possibility of a shower, it's way too cold anyway, but after so long the thought does cross my mind.

Pressure has dropped but very quickly and with sharp

jumps. I don't think it is another low and the forecast is clear but a worry just the same. Winds have veered from Northeast-East-South in just a matter of hours. Just enough wind to overpower the seas and keep the sails full. The motion is horrible as each wind change brings about a new set of wave directions making my world bounce in every direction. Sparrow seems to just act as if she doesn't care and plows right over everything.

I am amazed that the winds are so variable this far South. I never would have guessed anything but heavy West winds. If I've learned one thing over the last few months in the Southern Ocean, nothing is constant down here. Well maybe just the threat of getting a real bashing when a system rolls over but from where and when is anyone's guess. The forecast changes so fast and can't be counted on at all anymore. I just can't wait to get out of this place.

I made the decision to see about a supply drop at the Falkland's. I am sure I will never make it to Gloucester no matter how many fish I can catch. I figured I could get a sneaky food drop from one of my Caribbean fly-bys in Dominica or the BVI but if I am planning on that then why wait? I want cookies and chocolate and ham and cheese and bread, dear God bread!!! So, Jim is on the case and trying to see what is possible, I can only imagine the phone calls he is making right now.

Chapter 23
Ever East

The seas following Cyclone Irving had become more triangle shaped than I had ever experienced. Each peak throwing a spray of white crest into the air. A churning, messy sea in almost no wind is a very strange experience. The sound of waves slapping both near and far all come together in a clatter that can only be heard because of the lack of wind. The sight is amazing as well. Waves breaking for no reason while Sparrow was getting tossed in all directions. Unable to do anything, I lashed the tiller, dropped the sails, and endured.

With a few rain squalls I was able to catch 2 gallons of salt free water. The winds steadily filled back in and by noon we had made 156 miles, not bad considering the few hours that we didn't move an inch! The wind had come around to the West, and under the reefed mainsail and staysail the furthest off the wind I could sail was South East. I was exhausted and wanted nothing more than to be heading due East and dead down wind. In all the thousands of miles Sparrow and I had sailed together I had never been able to get good speed and a steady heading while sailing dead down wind. Mongo couldn't hold the course even when using a pole to steady the staysail. We never could get into a groove on that point of sail. So, I had settled to heading on a broad reach, not in the right direction but close. I was down below in my bunk trying to get some sleep, but every so often the staysail would collapse and then slam when the wind filled the sail. A very jarring and annoying sound when trying to sleep. It is also the shock load of a sail slamming that can break equipment faster than anything.

With a grunt and more than one expletive, I went on deck and started to play with the sails. I eased the mainsail as far out as possible and sheeted home the staysail. After adjusting Mongo to about 20 degrees off the wind we sailed. The staysail would slat but the mainsail stayed full and we started to surf the swell, controlled and steady. The next step was to lower the staysail and see if we could still hold our downwind course. Each wave coming from astern would lift us up and we would slide along with it for a few seconds. I waited, watched and tuned Mongo. I was sure that something would go wrong and Sparrow would lose control, resulting in an uncontrolled jibe. Wave after wave passed and Sparrow surfed and held a fine course the whole time! The only drawback was that the rolling motion was impressive to say the least, 30 degrees on each side. I didn't care, we were heading due East and moving well. My mood was completely turned around. I had a new weapon to deal with the rest of the Southern Ocean. I wondered how this new trick will work in a blow?

My whole life I have been a star gazer. The winters in Northern Michigan produce some of the most spectacular starry nights I have ever seen. The open ocean is the only place on earth where I have found brighter stars. The night of January 14th was different. With no moon and not a cloud in the sky, I was taking a quick look on deck before heading to my bunk when I noticed just how lit up Sparrow was. When I realized it was the brilliance of the stars alone that lit the deck, and even exposed the horizon, I changed my plans. My experience since rounding Good Hope had been of overcast skies and cloudy nights. I could only guess that Irving had stolen every cloud and bit of moisture in the air. What I was left with were the brightest stars I had ever seen in my life, at least twice as bright as the coldest night in Michigan. I made a huge cup of coffee and settled in the cockpit for the next few hours.

I was finding that another great part of sailing with the wind was that the cockpit and foredeck stayed relatively dry. I was riding my emotional rollercoaster to the highest peak. Shooting stars came and went, satellites flew in abundance and looked more like planes ripping across the sky. I thought about the great sights from Mother Nature that I had seen so far on the voyage. The sunsets in the Doldrums, the whales flanking Sparrow, and now this celestial show. All mine and mine alone. One fact that I couldn't escape was that the only way to see these wonders was to be out here. I was learning that suffering through so much was indeed worth it.

Father and son on day 133 of the Appalachian Trail

Mighty Sparrow hauled out at Knight Marine

1st Mate Adam on the sail to Gloucester

Bill preparing his famous blueberry pancakes

The water maker in full operation

Deep in the South Pacific Ocean

The Falkland Islands food drop

Three months of rationing

The sails come down for the last time. June 30th, 2018 after 271 days and 29,805 miles.

On solid ground for the first time in a long time!

Chapter 24
Stop and Go Sailing

-January 15th, 2018 Journal:

I got rain!!! So glad, 15 gallons! I am set for a good while now, was down to single digits and getting worried. Under the flash of distant lightning I scrambled around the deck collecting with every jug, pot, and cup aboard. I get to eat some dehydrated food tonight! Finally, something different. I can also hydrate with a double ration, maybe my pee will be less like soup!-

As we crossed over 40 degrees South latitude our position was just about 1,000 miles to the West South West of Cape Leeuwen in Western Australia. Catching so much rain would be about the only good thing that would happen for the rest of our time in the wide-open Indian Ocean. The further South we sailed the more extreme the weather became. The winds would come up for a day and then drop off the next. Always bringing with it the waves and swell.

The miles would fall behind us for a period and then just as fast as the winds rose, they would drop to the point that the mainsail would slat and inevitably have to come down. As this cycle became more pronounced it began to drive me to fits of rage. With nothing but the Southern Ocean around us, it became the focus of my anger. It is hard to express the frustration that fell over me every time the wind eased and the sails came down. The rolling motion causing the clatter of shifting stores, Colonel Clink banging away in the mast, and me gripping and wedging myself into any space that might be comfortable for a few hours. This went on and on from January 16th through the 22nd.

By January 23rd we passed 425 miles to the South of Cape Leeuwen Australia, our second of the Five Southern Capes! The only thing missing from the ceremony was the toast, as I had gone through all the booze on board, with the exception of a single beer that I intended to save for Cape Horn. It did, however, feel great to see the flags flying after more than a month since Good Hope. My thoughts turned to Buzz and I wondered just what he would do in these conditions? And what would he think of how I was handling myself?   I often find that when I reflect on the endurance and resolve of the people I hold in high regard, it somehow brings my spirits up, whether I want to emulate them or just take their accomplishments as an example. Either way, Buzz helped to get me out of my depression and keep me pushing forward. The weather forecast was also a big help.

Chapter 25
Ships Log

1800 April 5th, 2018
Lat 54 44'S, Long 075 18'W
Miles from Cape Horn: 355
Days at Sea: 186

Squalls and more Squalls all day, no rest for the weary. But for now, bring them on as I am catching rain and hail in each one, almost 5 gallons today! My hands are really taking a beating from the sail changes and then the hail scooping. I wish I could still use the scuba gloves!

Seas are becoming more and more unsettled with every squall. 20-30 minutes between blows but the wind seems to be holding even after each squall passes. Winds are fluctuating from F-6 to F-8 but all from the West so it is the 2nd reef that is pushing us along. I worry about the gusts but Sparrow seems to love them, I think we both want the same thing, to get free of the Southern Ocean.

Cracked open the last can of Peaches in celebration! The food drop will be ready in the Falkland's and I don't even need to stop. They will bring it out and toss boxes over to me, what a relief, I thought for sure I would have to at least tie up and clear customs. My trip will remain nonstop! All we have to do is get there, less than 300 miles to the Horn and then a week to the food. East ho Sparrow!

Chapter 26
On the Wind

I like to think that it was the passing of Cape Leeuwen that brought about the change in the weather. Or maybe finally getting free of the volatile Indian Ocean. By the end of January, the winds had become more consistent. In Southern Ocean terms this means that the low-pressure systems were much closer together with very little time in between. One after another they rolled over us and pushed Sparrow ever East and further South. Our daily miles were 125, 102, 138, 114, 143, 128, 120, 141, 127, 132, 132, 130, and 139. We were sailing better than at any other time thus far on the voyage and it felt great. The winds were shifting from South to West as each system passed over and the seas followed suit but never became overwhelming.

For the most part Sparrow only needed the mainsail in the West winds. Although we rolled constantly, the miles fell in our wake day after day. When the winds came around from the South the staysail was added for some extra speed and stability. I had modified the spinnaker pole to be able to pole out the staysail to prevent it from slamming when we sailed on a deep broad reach. Day and night, we sailed on. The chart that I was marking at this point was from Western Australia to Tasmania, covering a smaller area than the previous charts. We flew across this chart compared to the others that covered entire oceans. I was also able to catch rain almost every time the winds did their shift from West to South. Never more than a few gallons but it was always needed to replenish my supply. All in all, life was good for the weeks below Australia.

My mental state was breaking away from the worries and frustration since entering the Southern Ocean in December. Although the challenges would never cease, I was becoming more confident in Sparrow's and my ability to keep going. I was still riding my rollercoaster of emotion that went up and down with the conditions of the sea, but I was also starting to think that I could make it home. To be honest, I never gave myself very good odds for success. Whether it be the boat breaking down or my mind not handling the rough weather. So many things could end a trip of this magnitude. So far nothing had, and when problems did arise, we handled them and kept pushing forward.

Early on January 29th I was snapped from a dream by the slamming mainsail. Like so many times before, I uttered a few expletives and put on my damp wet weather gear to head on deck. If ever there was a time that I was glad I didn't just say to hell with it and stayed in my bunk, it was this day. The sky was as angry as I had ever seen it. Massive black squalls were all around. The squall just down wind of us had let loose its rain and killed the wind. The next squall behind us had a different appearance from what I was used to seeing, as if the cloud was just a solid wall from sea to sky. The temperature was in the low 40's and I could see my own breath. As the squall approached it didn't look like anything I had seen before.

Normal squalls all look very much the same. A big fluffy cloud with a dark patch of rain just beneath it. Sometimes the winds were very strong and other times it just rained. I was getting very good at guessing which was about to overtake us, but this was an oddball. The cloud was fluffy on top but just kept its white wall all the way to the surface of the sea. Almost like a fog bank if not for the height of the cloud. I dropped the mainsail and had only the staysail up. The wind was nonexistent so nothing much changed. As the winds hit, they increased to over

40 knots in seconds. The surprise came in the form of marble sized hail stones! Accelerated by the winds, I was pinned down behind the dodger and just holding on. The balls made a huge clatter on deck and collected very fast. In 5 minutes, the squall had passed, and I sat on deck looking at my hail covered boat.

There was nothing I could have done during the squall, mostly because I couldn't have looked at anything for fear of taking a hail stone in the eye. But once again, Sparrow stood up to the conditions and shook it off like so many times before. I spent the next half hour trying to locate the ski goggles I had brought from home. I had both clear and tinted lenses and stowed them close to the Nav station for easy access. I wanted to be ready for the next round of hail.

As January ended, we were still over 500 miles West of Tasmania at about 44 degrees South latitude. I had hopes of sailing close and looking at the land, but as the winds dictated my fastest heading, I was once again in the hands of Mother Nature. Intermixed with the train of low-pressure systems were more hail squalls, normal squalls, and calms. Rain was being caught a few gallons at a time until a new threat arrived, one that I had seen before this voyage but had forgotten about until now.

Over the years of sailing primarily in the Atlantic, I had seen a few waterspouts drop out of very dark clouds. Basically a tornado at sea, I always believed that they were relegated to the tropical areas of the world's oceans. Not so. January 27th, a day like any other, sails would go up and down with the squalls and progress was difficult. Out of the west came a very dark, very wide cloud line. Like a snake falling out of a tree, the grey tube of the waterspout left the cloud and touched the sea. It was a few miles off but the squall line was heading right toward us. I watched the spout as it would twist its way to the sea and then, as if being shocked, it would retreat to the sky. As the pulsing continued, I started to wonder just what could be done if we were to be hit. I figured all sails down, dodger lashed, and anything on deck lashed as well. Maybe 10 minutes of work was my best guess and I grabbed spare lines ready to do the lashing if need be. Then I just sat and watched. Thankfully, the waterspout vanished before the squall line reached us.

The last big blow from the series of low-pressure systems came on January 30th. Winds strengthened from the South West and we flew along. In a matter of hours, the seas became gigantic and breaking. Sparrow surfed for what seemed like minutes at a time under the 3rd reefed mainsail and staysail. I was pushing her a little harder than usual, as my proximity to land gave me confidence that if something were to break, I would be able to get to Australia, Tasmania or New Zealand. The moon came out, almost full, and gave me even more confidence to sail harder. With the world around us lit up, giving squalls no place to hide, I just set my alarm for 1-hour increments and carried through the night faster than ever before.

The sounds of waves breaking around us was becoming more and more pronounced. Sparrow was playing with the waves and getting in some of the best surfing of her life. The high point was an incredible surge, first down and then forward. Normally, I would see up to 14 or 15 knots on the GPS, but a glance over and 19.5 knots was the peak speed. Imagine that! Sparrow, a 44-year-old boat surfing at nearly 20 knots; so much for the nickname "Wet Snail!" Her long keel keeping us stable, and Mongo handling the wind changes, we would be blanketed from the wind in the trough of each wave. The team was working well and giving this ocean a run for its money.

I can only figure that we were working our way through a countercurrent. The winds never exceeded F-8 and shouldn't have built the waves up so much. But add in a 1-2 knot current going against the wind and the effect is very dramatic. The whole night was something out of a movie with the moonlight reflecting off of the breaking waves. I was careful to keep the seas about 30 degrees off the stern as I didn't want a repeat of the knockdown near Cyclone Irving. The night faded away and just before sunrise, the winds fell off, as I knew they would.

Chapter 27
Off the Wind at the 3rd Cape

The next five days were a mix of madness, hope, and let down. The winds toyed with us as the seas set Sparrow into a motion that was enough to bring about many screaming matches between me and ocean. The currents were adding to our daily miles but the winds would not stay steady for more than a few hours at a time. This added to my work and my frustration. Day and night the winds would pick up and sails would be reefed. Then the sound of the mainsail slamming would wake me up and I would add more sail; over and over.

Just a week before I had been howling at the moon and on an emotional high well above anything so far on the trip. Now I was very low. Thinking only of my family and friends, I became extremely lonely out on the ocean. I was also becoming more and more worried about how far South we were, 47 degrees South latitude and there to stay. With no room to head North of an approaching low-pressure system, I always felt most vulnerable when sailing under the Capes. My thought was to get around into the Pacific quietly and head a bit North nearer to 40 degrees South latitude. I could not do that now, not until I had passed the 3rd Cape, Tasmania, but also the 4th, New Zealand; a distance of nearly 1,000 miles.

On February 3rd the flags again went up, and Buzz went overboard. A view of Tasmania was not happening as we sailed 160 miles South of the Southernmost point of the island. It felt great, as usual, to see the flags come out. All in great condition, as they spent only a few hours flying each time I performed the ceremony. "Hail to the Victors" filled the air not once but three times in tribute to the 3rd Cape. The winds were filling in and rain was falling down as we finally sailed out of the Indian Ocean and into the South Tasman Sea.

The speech I gave to the Indian Ocean is not worth repeating verbatim. More expletives than other words flew from my mouth. What a terrible place. Calms and storms, thirst and worries. I was beyond glad to be free after nearly 50 days trying my best to get across that awful stretch of ocean. I vowed never to return to the South Indian Ocean again.

Chapter 28
Ships Log

1900 April 6th, 2018
Lat 55 32'S, Long 072 34'W
Miles from Cape Horn: 250
Days at Sea:187

Winds are constantly changing and that means sail changes. I never sleep, I just can't. I am too close to the Horn and have to take advantage of every gift of wind I am given. 2 hours sleep in the last 24 hours but I am sure it added 10 or 20 extra miles. On the Pacific chart it was nothing but on this little chart of Cape Horn that's almost an Inch! We move so fast on this chart I can't help but plot my position more often. A small squall woke me at 4 am, cold and snowing. The wind dropped for 2 hours and then filled in enough to get me back to my bunk. I am so tired but excited as well.

Feeling very positive now that I am eating more, thank you Jim! I can feel the food giving me energy and keeping me warm in the snow and freezing temperatures. I wonder just how much weight I have lost since rationing began South of Australia? I have not seen myself in almost two months, I just add more thermal layers to fight off the cold.

Flat becalmed for maybe the 20th time in three days! This terrible ocean, just let me go. I tried to rest but I can only sit and wait for the winds to return. Finally, around 2200 the wind returned with a crisp F-5 from the West. So close now and wide awake. I feel like I am being watched. This close to the greatest of all Capes I feel very out of place, I shouldn't be here, I don't think any sailor should.

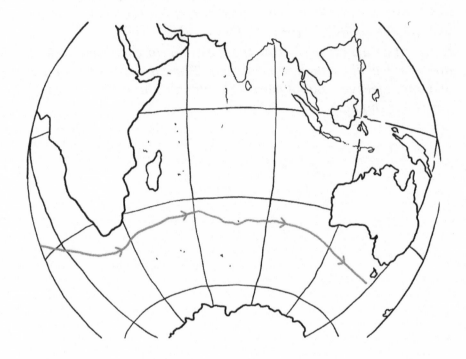

Chapter 29
South Tasman Gale

    With the Indian Ocean in our wake we were becalmed once more on a rolling sea. It was time for a full check of Sparrow and my ship stores. On deck, the biggest problem I ran into was the lashing lines hanging from the forward rail. The three strands lines that are braided together were coming apart. It seemed as though both Sparrow and I were both growing beards! Like wispy white hairs on an old man's chin, about 20 thin, braided lines dangle from the shrouds to the end of the bow sprit. If I reduce the head sail, I don't have to un-hank and stow the sail, I can just lower it and lash the sail to the life line. Much less work and the sail is ready to fly in a moment's notice. The only time I will remove the sail is to change which head sail I am using. Otherwise, if rough weather is coming, a big enough wave could rip the sail or even break the lifeline.

Back down below, I once again counted the food stores; just over 300 servings left. I knew then where I went wrong. When ordering the food packets and freeze-dried goods, I was counting servings as meals. In a normal day, I would have wanted about 3 servings per meal to satisfy my hunger. But with the numbers staring me right in the face I had no choice but to ration down to 3 servings a day and hope like hell I could finish this trip in 100 days! Fresh water had been getting a boost of a few gallons every other day or so since we sailed past Cape Leeuwen. Still never more than 20 gallons on board at any time, but way better than 2 gallons total, my all-time low! Otherwise Sparrow was in fine shape as the winds began to fill in and the pressure began to drop.

The seas had changed color dramatically, going from a cold steal blue to emerald green. Lots of sea life was being kicked around so close to land with all the strange currents. At night I would shine my torch in the water and see thousands of glowing little eyes looking back at me. I figured they were shrimp or squid. After a minute I cut the light, as my imagination ran toward what else could be just under the surface. I wanted to slip by unnoticed, not attract any unwanted attention. In the morning, I watched a lone Albatross, the biggest I had seen, glide between the waves without a single flap of its 10-foot wingspan. For half an hour I watch as this giant of the sky circled us, very curious about Sparrow's sail, or just hoping that some food will pop up in our wake. I had heard that they can sometimes sleep while flying. I guessed that out on the open ocean it might be safer than floating on the water, but I had seen many birds just bobbing on the waves. It is incredible to watch them. No matter the conditions, there are always birds and I was glad to have the company.

-February 5th, 2018 Journal:

Wind and sea have built up during the night. Finally, out of my bunk as the sound of the increasing winds wake me and tell me to go take a look. Wow, things are much bigger now. The pressure dropped another 5 bars in the past few hours. I have the staysail and 3rd reef in the mainsail flying. Sparrow is galloping over the waves just off the wind. She moves through the breakers well and with great speed but if conditions become worse, we could be in trouble. I can't head further off the wind with the staysail still up so down it must come.

I made my way to the foredeck, clinging to everything with both hands and feet, one eye on the boat and the other on approaching waves. A quick job and back to the security of the cockpit. I give Mongo a few clicks to fall off the wind and waves a bit more. This took the sting out of the wind and though we were rolling heavily we also surfed. My hands are freezing so down below for hot coffee.

The glass has steadied so now I just wait. The seas are still building and squalls start rolling in. Some of the waves are over 40 feet now and coming from two directions. Sparrow is doing well so far. In the squalls the wind kicks up the sea spray all over our world. Just holding on now and hoping things will ease up. Just about lost everything with one big breaker from the South! Peering out from the companionway hatch I caught sight of a monster wall of green water. Much bigger than the rest and forming a clear tip as it prepared to break. I slammed the hatch and jumped to the Nav station and held on. Sparrow rose up and then right back down. The world went quiet for a second and another look through the hatch revealed that the wave broke just a few feet passed us and left behind a patch of white bubbling sea a few hundred feet long. A close call, lucky once again.

The storm is passing and the glass is up 3 bars now. Too dark to see anything but the glowing breakers from the phosphorescent. I want to set more sail but I am exhausted from the stress of the day and the squalls keep coming every 30 minutes or so. All I want is to take a break but it's impossible right now.-

I had been warned by Adam that I was entering some very strong countercurrents and eddies as we sailed into the South Tasman Sea. As the waves built up, I sent him a message to find out what was going on with our position. The waves were incredible and developed so fast that it had to be current related. All I received was that I was in a bad spot with an almost 2 knot current coming from the East, directly opposing the Westerly gale. My only question was how long until I was free? The reply came quickly; 24 hours! I am sure to Adam, sitting in a warm house, 24 hours seemed like good news, no time at all. In my world that was going to be an eternity. Violently rolling and pitching in huge waves, with random giants roaming around and surely looking for that little boat that dared to sail around the world.

I was mad at my brother for letting me sail into this countercurrent. Why had he not told me to go North or South to avoid it? I was looking for anything to blame for what was going on aboard Sparrow during the gale. Any excuse to say, "well to hell with this, not my fault, I'm heading for New Zealand." The thought of giving up was running wild in my head as the world tossed us around. How many more of these storms could we take? How many more could I take?

In the morning cooler heads prevailed, and I realized that I had just been scared and tired and stressed for so long. I also felt badly for my negative thoughts toward Adam. But I was blessed with a wind that had eased, but not blown out completely as I had expected. We sailed on for the day, and as the seas calmed and became more comfortable, I went about getting cleaned up from all the salt on me and in the cabin. My socks came off for the first time in weeks, soaking wet for the last 24 hours. My feet were quite a sight. I actually reeled back in my chair when I saw the layers of wrinkled white skin. The calluses that I had built up over years of a barefoot life in the Caribbean were falling off in chunks. My toenails were longer than I had ever seen outside of pictures. Curving down the front of my toes and covered with lint from the socks.

I will save the fine details of my grooming over the next hour but will say that it was more rewarding than anything I had ever experienced on the Appalachian Trail! Next up I needed to sort out what was blocking up the faucet from my fresh water. A small filter under the sink was taken out, and to my surprise, was filled with a grey sludge. I still have no idea what this was, but in the tanks, a light grey cloud floated around. It must have been some sort of bacteria, and though the filter caught most of it, I am sure plenty was getting into each drink I took. A drop of bleach in each tank would have to suffice as I had no other way to clean the water. I hadn't felt any effect from drinking the water, so I wasn't too worried.

The winds filled in from the North and became steady for more than two days, something I was not used to at all in the Southern Ocean. I slept as much as possible and had very vivid dreams about friends, family and food. One dream had me in a gas station leaning over a full freezer of premade ice-cream cones. Reaching in with all the delight in the world, just as I had one in my hand, I woke up. I was so disappointed that for the next hour or so I tried desperately to fall back to sleep and get that ice cream! Unable to do so I gave up in a huff and went on deck and fell into a deep depression. It is strange, but the littlest things can do that when you are alone at sea for a long time. It was about time I took a long look into my brain to see how things were going.

I am no psychologist but I have poked around my mind plenty in my life. Many nights spent on watch doing yacht deliveries, and especially my time on the Appalachian Trail, afforded me more than my share of introspection. On this trip I had promised myself that I would not look back over my past. I wanted to be in the moment, and spending my days going over my past life would distract me from this adventure. I would, however, allow for a bit of each day to think of the future. Mostly daydreaming about being back home and what I would do during the summer in Michigan.

I wondered about how much I was talking to myself,

Sparrow and Mongo. The three amigos. I figure it was totally normal in my current circumstances to do this. I wasn't hearing any response besides the normal creaks and groans you always hear at sea. My most convincing rationalization I came up with was that it would have been far stranger to not say a word for the last few months. Only a crazy person could pull that off!

As we approached New Zealand the winds eased, and we flew more and more sail. Day and night with full canvas up. I was always worried about sleeping in the Southern Ocean with full sail, so I slept very little and watched as my coffee supply dwindled. On February 9th, a few squalls came in and I was able to catch 7 gallons of rain before the winds died completely. All sails down and the sun began its plunge to the horizon.

At first just a yellow line above the sea, I sat on deck for the coming sunset. The majority have been covered in clouds and as they became less frequent, I never missed out. Within a few minutes the sky turned a bright orange, bleeding into a deep red off to the West and illuminating a whale a few hundred feet astern as it blew its spout a few times. Enjoying the scene, I almost would have missed out on the Eastern horizon if I had not turned around to make another cup of coffee. A double rainbow as bright as any I had seen and stretching unbroken from end to end. All of which was cast in a brilliant orange.

Complete amazement fell over me as I spun in circles to take in as much of my world as possible. I wanted time to freeze and just live forever in this eerie half-light, but the sky fell deeper red and the rainbows disappeared slowly from each end until meeting in the middle. The colors of the sky were soon replaced with the brightest of the planets and stars until they filled the newly speckled sky. The gentle roll of Sparrow; for once the motion was not too bad; sent me into a deep sleep that night. The gale, the waves, the steady North winds and then this sunset. All things were good in my world. With a little luck I would be sighting land the very next day.

Chapter 30
Land Ho!

February 10th was the last day spent sailing in the Tasman Sea before heading off into the wide open South Pacific Ocean. By noon we had only covered 78 miles in the calm conditions. For the first time, the winds swung around from the East and we were stopped dead in our wake. Mighty Sparrow is many things but an upwind sailboat she is not. The only way to take any advantage of the Easterly wind was to take the day off and set a course for the Snares. This odd group of uninhabited islands lies about 60 miles South of Stewart Island, New Zealand. Truly a no-man's land if there ever was one. Two sets of rocky outcrops that rise a few hundred feet above the ocean. Just the name alone conjures images of a place that most sailboats would avoid, but for me I longed to see something on the horizon besides the rolling swell.

I had contacted Mike Porter about how close I could sail to the islands as my chart only showed two dots the size of a grain of sand. "All clear" was the quick response. "The cliffs just drop right off and it's deep water all around." Glad to have this assurance, we approached with reduced sails and under clear skies. Within a mile I was getting a better idea of how massive the islands were. A fog bank rolled in and suddenly the world was shrouded in a white curtain that added to the prehistoric feel of the place. Speckled by green moss and white bird droppings, the cliffs rose dramatically from the ocean. Sea birds circled around us and seals followed in our wake. We passed large kelp beds streaming with the current. The smell, while not wonderful from the abundance of bird life, was still the smell of earth. After so many days in the fresh, almost sterile air of the open ocean, the smell of land hit me like a brick wall.

Back and forth we slowly sailed about a quarter mile from shore and in the lee of the building Easterly winds. I had no big storms coming and no change in the wind direction for at least 48 hours. This would be the one "Day Off" of the whole trip. The one time that I was not pressing forward and trying to gain miles. The constant effort of always pushing forward just drifted away as I gazed, without blinking, at these storied islands.

Many ships had sailed to their doom because of the Snares in the great age of sailing 200 years before. Caught in bad weather and unsure of their position. I imagined what it must have been like aboard a tall ship sailing from Australia or the East Indies, fully loaded with goods and needing to thread the needle between the Snares and Auckland Island, another 100 miles to the South. No position fix for days and the waves starting to heap up as the sea floor begins to shallow. And then the dreaded scream of land ho! But it's too late and the breakers take the men and ship on a cold stormy night. Just to see the waves of a storm pound into the cliffs would be quite a sight. 60 to 80-foot waves bashing into the gnarled, rocky islands. I wondered, but at the same time was so glad to arrive on a calm day, just lucky to see the islands I had always wanted to sight when planning the trip.

My thoughts drifted back to the years that the three Ocean Passage Planning Charts were spread out on a table at my parents' house. Jim and I meeting secretly after dinner to go over the route I would take. Not wanting to upset my Mother, who was still hoping that my plan to sail around the world was just a dream and not really going to happen. For some reason, my finger would always pause at the Snares. Something in the name I guess, I only hoped that I would see them some day. And now I was looking directly at them.

After many wonderful hours in the sight of land, with the winds still from the East, we made our way North. Just visible was Stewart Island on the horizon. A land I know all too well. I had spent 10 days hiking around the island and over its mountains with Adam and my cousin Nick. We were only there because my Father had spent some time there in the 1960's just after college. The punishing trails, mud- bogs, mountains, wind and rain. Just the right place for backpacking off the beaten track. The memories flooded back; I sent a message to both with news of my view.

Still not quite in the Pacific Ocean, we had two more dangers to negotiate; North and South Trap. Two rocky reefs just under the water and able to end a sailing trip without a thought. By sunset, with nothing but open water ahead, we entered the Pacific Ocean! After a night of calms and shifts the winds slowly came in from the North on February 12th, and we had made only 25 miles noon to noon. Rain came and went and so did the winds. The one worry I had was the pressure, 988 bars and falling still, a slow fall over days but never a great sign to see the needle pointed so low.

As we entered the Pacific Ocean my water supply was floating at a comfortable 20 gallons, food was being counted regularly and looked a little concerning, but Sparrow was still strong as ever. We were heading into the last unknown ocean, but before it was official, the flags went up and Buzz went over on February 13th. The fourth of the great Southern Capes had been passed. It is hard to believe that we only needed to cross the Pacific and round Cape Horn before turning North and truly heading for home. But to make it there, to the South Atlantic, we had to cross the largest expanse of open ocean on the planet. The last unmarked ocean chart was unrolled on the Nav station. It looked huge, the largest scale chart I owned. Over 4,000 miles to the Horn with the Southern Ocean summer coming to a close. One thing was for sure, it was going to be a tough sail ahead.

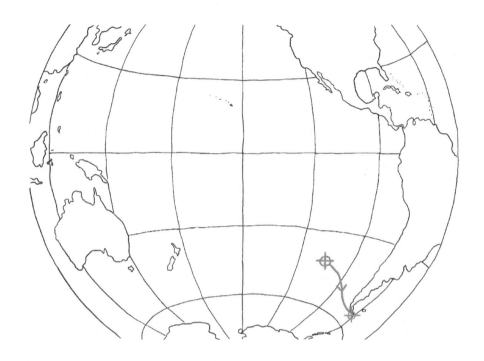

Chapter 31
Ships Log

April 7th, 2018
Lat 55 53'S, Long 070 52'W
Miles from Cape Horn: 137
Days at Sea:188

 Dumb move on my part. Around 0200 a big wind shift sent me on deck in the snow. Steaming mad I got out of my bunk. Confused and tired I accidently jibed and then jibed again to get back on track but did so out of anger and without thinking. The impact broke the VHF antenna clean off the spreader and was dangling by its coax cable. Half way up the mast I went but could only manage to wedge it against the mast with the halyards. Once we get in the lee of the Horn, I can do a proper job of fixing it.

Winds are steady at dawn and a quick check on deck gives me a full 5 gallons of freezing cold fresh water, the temperature is about 28 degrees and stings my nose. A small Cape Pidgin is huddled in the cockpit and I leave it be, I figure we are in this together. Back down below and time for some steaming hot powdered mash, my body is void of any warmth right now but I am so close to the Horn I just don't care about anything but getting around and heading North.

More Squalls rolling in with less punch but adding to the F-7 winds from the South. The seas are sloppy and dangerous and I don't want to go on deck at all. We are down to the 3rd reef and staysail for now. Less than 100 miles to go!

Like a switch the winds are now at F-8 and higher with squalls, all from the South West. The seas have changed from blue to purple and birds are everywhere. This is Cape Horn water, and getting to be like the weather I expected. I have to laugh at all the people who tried to predict my weather for this day. It will be calm they said, you have a great weather window! I told them to stop and not curse me, the last thing I want to do is upset whatever controls this terrible place. Let me sneak by, I won't tell a soul.

Land Ho! Isles Ildefonso ten miles on the port beam. Very cool to see land after so long, I would love to get closer but I have to hold on to the little sea room I have. If the wind and sea start raging, I will want to be able to run without hitting the Horn.

More hail squalls whipping the winds up into the 50's and we are down to storm sails and flying along. With the current we are holding 7-8 knots of boat speed! Go Sparrow Go! The forecast calls for the winds to ease as night falls and things don't seem to be intensifying so I try for a midday nap as I am sure it will be a long night.

A few minutes before midnight and the first lights of the 5th Cape have been sighted! Eight miles due North and that is Cape Horn. If only the clouds would part to give the half-moon a chance to show me the famous rock. Not a place to hang about so we press on and use the easing winds by adding more sail through the night but not before I have the one beer that I have saved for so many months! I am sure at the very least it will be ice cold!

Chapter 32
A Slow Start to the Big Ocean

I often took solace in reading the books of the first solo circumnavigators. They just seemed to have a much harder go of sailing in the Southern Ocean than my voyage. When conditions became unbearable, all I needed to do was turn to the chapter that coincided with where Sparrow and I were. I would read of the misery that they were dealing with compared to my own. More often than not I would put the book down and say, "well it could be worse I guess" with a laugh.

After clearing the islands and reefs that dot the seas South of New Zealand progress was horribly slow. The first week produced runs of 25, 51, 85, 65, 49 and 48 miles. Not one day close to what Sparrow could do with good winds and calm seas. The frustration and work involved to gain each and every one of those miles was reaching a boiling point. A breeze would come up and so all sail would fly. Then the swell would increase and roll Sparrow so hard that her sails couldn't grip the wind. The sails would fill and collapse over and over until I had to take them in and wait for conditions to change.

Rather than just stare at the sails and wait, I tried my best to occupy my mind and come up with anything to pass the time.

In the relatively shallow water we were in, a small tuna took the bait and was brought aboard with success. My fishing gear was very basic. A hand line coiled on a plastic spool. I would lead it overboard and cleat off the line. To protect my fingers from the line and the fish I wore an old pair of leather motorcycle gloves. This being the first fish caught since my rationing for the last few weeks, I took extra care to clean every bit of the delicious meat. I had brought along a good store of soy sauce and little tubs of wasabi. While preparing large pieces of meat for later cooking, I enjoyed the fresh taste of raw tuna less than 20 minutes from the sea. A treat only sailors and fishermen ever really get to enjoy. In all, that tuna provided 3 meals, not servings but full meals. Prepared with rice or lentils I was filling my stomach for the first time in a while.

The dining experience set my mind to taking a more realistic count of my provisions. 290 servings, some of which were just small packets of potatoes au gratin or the notorious RSPP's that made my stomach produce an unholy amount of gas. With a heavy heart, I knew at this point that I would not be able to make the trip all the way back to Gloucester without a supply drop. But where?

I must admit my first thought was where could I stop so that no one will ever find out. I wanted nothing more than to succeed in all the goals I set out to achieve. Never needing assistance was one of the major goals. I had friends in the Caribbean that could keep quiet for sure. And those islands would be easy to sail into under the cover of darkness. I couldn't imagine that I would get caught in Dominica or the BVI by the Customs Authority. Numbers of days, miles, and food servings flew through my head and then on to paper. Over and over I would try to calculate just how long I could stay at sea and ration what I had left. Fishing would be done every day when conditions were good, and depending on what I caught I figured I could make it to the Caribbean.

Sloppy cross seas and light winds continued. I reached deep into my sailing knowledge to try to keep Sparrow moving. Using the spinnaker pole with the staysail or jib, sailing at different angles against the waves, I tried anything that came to mind. We were in a race now. A race across the Pacific Ocean, but not against another boat. We raced the oncoming autumn gales and a dwindling food supply. No longer could I just wait out the conditions. We needed to make miles and make them at every opportunity possible.

Upon my morning inspection, I discovered two more rivet heads lying on the deck. They were coming from the mainsail track on the mast. All the slating of the mainsail was taking its toll. A closer look at the #3 jib and a few holes had appeared. These were all fixable problems but worrisome all the same. I sometimes felt guilt and shame when I discovered problems. Sparrow's job was to sail me around the world, my job was to take care of Sparrow and keep her happy and in good repair. When something broke because I let the sails slam or left a project unfinished, I felt terrible. But that feeling is also what prods me into action and brings out the tool box and sewing machine. With every fix I feel better, and always promise not to let the same problem happen again.

The winds continued to be light and variable day after day. Just to add a little suspense to my miserable life at this point, Cyclone Gita was growing in size and pummeling Fiji. The forecast track was taking the cyclone to New Zealand next and then just North of my position. My hope was that as it hit the cold waters, the storm would just fall apart. An offshore fishing boat called on the radio during the day of February 15th. After a few questions about just what the hell I was doing sailing to Cape Horn in this little boat, a long pause was brought on after hearing the number of days I had been at sea. Then they warned of the coming storm. Thankfully, the Captain's outlook was similar to mine, that the storm would either be weakened when it hit New Zealand or when it reached the cold waters of the Southern Ocean. This was music to my ears. "You should be alright but keep an eye on the weather for the next week," were the last words before signing off.

Another Cyclone heading my way, great! A repeat of Cyclone Irving in the Indian Ocean was the last thing I needed, though this storm was much larger and more dangerous. A look around the conditions and I realized it was just like Irving, light winds and a rolling swell that made keeping Sparrow moving very difficult if not impossible. For now, I would press on and fight my way East, but if we have to choose between cutting in front of the storm as we did before, or turning tail, I was not sure what we would do. I sure as hell needed to make miles and continue my race against time and hunger rather than turn to the West and wait things out.

Nevertheless, we pushed on as slow as ever, averaging only 2 knots of boat speed. Through banks of fog and constantly changing skies, the wind never rose above F-2. With the constant swell, there was just nothing that could be done. I kept the fishing line out but was finding that the only thing I was attracting was a crowd of sea birds. Eventually, I pulled the line in and found that the constant attack from sharp beaks was tearing the lure apart. Reaching the end of my rope and an area of shallow water that I figured was the best chance for catching a fish, I loaded the shotgun. My intent was not to kill the birds but just to scare them away from my lure. After a few rounds splashing into the sea the birds would leave for a few minutes and the gun would go below. Not 30 minutes later they were all back and so was the shotgun! This went on for the whole morning of February 17th and ended in tragedy.

Among the dive-bombing birds was one large Albatross. After a good volley of buck shot from me and a quick disappearance of the bird, I once again stowed the shotgun below. Just as I came back on deck the Albatross went into a dive and didn't come up. When it popped up to the surface, I could see that it was hooked! I reached for the line but it was as tight as a piano wire. From my view it looked as though this beautiful creature was being dragged, beak open and filling with sea water like a balloon. I rounded Sparrow up but in the few seconds of being dragged the Albatross was dead. As I pulled the line in it felt as though I was tugging on a flooded dinghy. I considered cutting the line but before I made a move the lure was free and the line went slack. It seemed that the Albatross had just gotten the hook under the curved end of her peak. What a waste of life and in such an empty place. I stowed the fishing line and broke down for a while thinking of what I had done. Surely, I would pay for that mistake. It is well known that the killing of an Albatross by a sailor has always brought about bad luck.

From then on, anytime I was fishing, if even one bird came in for a look, the line came in and was stowed. I could live with one death by mistake but a second would mean that I was just putting my own hunger above the life of an innocent animal. Besides, I did have food, not much but enough to not have to risk the lives of such beautiful creatures. As if to forgive this tragedy, the winds started to fill in as the Bounty Islands came into sight about 5 miles to the South. The pressure was jumping up and down from 990 to 1002 and back. Not as concerning as a steep drop, but unsettling all the same.

Just to the South the white covered hills of the Bounty Islands appeared and disappeared in the rolling Westerly swell. With the temperature around 50 degrees, I can only imagine how bad that Island would smell, as the white that covers most of its surface is definitely bird droppings. An impressive but unseen rock exploded with each passing swell about a mile offshore. I wanted nothing more than to guide Sparrow closer, but my intentions were never to linger. Thinking that this would be the only time in my life I would be this close, it was a battle in my mind. But with an impending Cyclone and the constant low-pressure systems this far South the name of the game was to always move East without delay.

For the first time in what seemed like an eternity Sparrow was finally sailing well, and the miles were disappearing under her keel. By noon on February 18th we had made our first good run in a week with 122 miles. Not just the miles, but the sailing was really wonderful. A very large gentle swell rolled under us from the West, a single wave direction was becoming rare as we were getting closer to 50 degrees South latitude. We normally had waves from the North, West and South. The winds were a steady F-4 from the North and in those conditions, Sparrow can really put on a show. As each roller picked us up, we would surge forward up to 8 or 9 knots and then drop back to 4 or 5 knots as we fell down the passing wave. Without the curse of a cross sea or any wind chop to speak of, the sailing was so rhythmic it put me into a trance. I can sit for hours on the foredeck and just stare out at the passing waves.

Part of what was producing the beautiful wave pattern was the fact that I was in relatively shallow water as we sailed over the Bounty Plateau. We were lucky to have the calm conditions, as this can become a very dangerous place in a gale. For so long I had been worrying about what could come out of the West at any time, the ink black clouds that I had read so much about and seen myself a few times thus far. I was never too comfortable no matter what the conditions or the forecast foretold. In the 2 months that we have been sailing in the Southern Ocean, I don't think I had truly relaxed once. A constant weight presses down on a sailor in the high latitudes. The fear of the storm that cannot be weathered.

At 1900 we sailed over an imaginary line and into a time warp, the International Date Line. Flags up and Buzz over! I wondered if the currents were just right, maybe a bit of Buzz would end up on one of the Bounty Islands. He really would have loved to be able to lay his eyes on these places that I have seen. The last time I saw Buzz was at a lunch in Michigan before returning to the Bitter End for my final season. Buzz had made the comment to my Father that I was doing the thing that they had always dreamed of doing. All he wanted to do was ask questions about the preparation and planning leading up to the trip. It made me feel good to have a man that was such an inspiration from my childhood so interested in my own adventure. When I learned of his passing a few months later, the first thought in my mind was how glad I was to have made sure not to let anything get in the way of that lunch. It is so easy to pass up spending time with friends and family on the promise to meet another day. Alone at sea, I thought often about things like that.

As far as the technical aspects of passing from the Eastern

to the Western hemisphere, I was not sure what I needed to do. We had passed through some 17 times zones, and when I remembered, I would set the clock forward an hour usually about every week or 10 days. If the sun started to rise around 0400, I knew I was a little late in my time change. But for the Date Line I was sure I needed to do something more drastic, but what? Since the Sextant had been securely stored for the rest of the Southern Ocean, I didn't really need to have the exact time, or day, for that matter. So, I just kept going and doing my normal routine without much worry. My clock and calendar lay in the Sun, Moon and Stars, although they have been stolen most days by thick cloud cover or fog. This far along we needed nothing more to make our waypoint; Cape Horn.

Chapter 33
Ships Log

1600 April 8th, 2018
Lat 55 50's, Long 066 17'W
Days at Sea: 189

No luck with the moon. After enjoying my time at the Cape I was able to get a few hours of sleep with plenty of sea room to ease my mind and being tired from the stressful day leading to the Horn. Woke up to the motion of small waves instead of big swell! For the first time in many months I am in the lee of the land, I have looked forward to this day for so long. Job done and now it's time to get North.

Up before the sun and time for a weather check. The winds are dying off and before I know it the sails are down, I am drifting with the current. Though it won't last for long as the next system is coming in with North West winds.

A ship! The first I have seen since the fishermen near the Bounty Islands almost two months ago. No AIS signal so my broken VHF antenna really is broken! I have the spare and get moving to install it before I lose this ship and can't test that it works. I ran all the wires and presto, there is the ship on my little screen, I can only guess that the coax cable to the VHF antenna has rubber through somewhere. Just as long as they can see me, I am happy.

Tried to start the engine to get a little charge to the batteries but no luck. I know she hates to start in cold weather but I am planning to bleed the fuel system and change the fuel filter. I just hope for a little sun to bring the charge up enough to really give it a go. I fear the batteries are beyond repair by now. Undercharged for over three months is not good.

Changed my contact lenses this morning. What a difference! Seems like a whole new world now that I have made it round the Horn. All new everything! Just trying to make it here I have been holding out before changing anything and soon enough I will be able to clean myself and Mighty Sparrow, what a day that will be.

Winds are up from the North West and we beat hard into small chop. Living on a 20-degree heel is not so bad when the swell is gone. I can even cook some rice, most of all I can relax a little! I have the 3rd reef in the mainsail just to take the edge off, I plan to get some real sleep if the weather holds.

Chapter 34
Cyclone Gita

The perfect winds that were so enjoyable, and which gave Sparrow and me a huge boost in both morale and miles, soon ended. My piece of mind was shattered when a fog bank rolled over us the very next day. Taking our wind and replacing it with a strong cross swell from the North, the sails stayed up and slammed violently. I normally would have taken them in, but with the wisps of clear air I thought it would soon pass. We pitched and rolled and I listened to the angry sails. I couldn't believe it, again we were becalmed! The screaming and yelling went on until I finally dropped all sail and stewed in the cockpit. I am not sure what or why I was so incensed. I had been becalmed so many times that I should have been used to this by now. Maybe I was just reaching the end of my patience, or feeling the looming threat of Cyclone Gita. Either way I went down below to look once more at the forecast.

The forecast model was telling me that I was in a good 15-20 knots of wind from the North. By the end of the day it will swing around to the West South West and strengthen. A look on deck told a very different story. Maybe it was the frustration brought on by expecting one thing, and getting something completely different and not even close to what I wanted. I was steaming mad, and with smoke coming out of my ears I went to update the forecast for the second time in as many days. I hit the power button and the screen blinked, the power light blinked and all went black. The hairs stood upright on my arms and a chill shot through my body. "Do not tell me this is happening," was all I could utter.

I had two computers aboard but my old one, the one I had been using for the weather downloads for almost two years, had just stopped working. I checked the battery, tried turning it back on after 10 minutes and then messaged Adam for help. All the while Sparrow wallowed with a motion that felt like a childhood group of bullies had encircled me and were pushing me around in different directions. A few tips came back from Adam and I tried them all, but nothing worked. I went on deck and lost my emotions for a second time on the trip. In my mind, all I could think of was what it would be like to have to cross the Pacific and round Cape Horn without being able to see the weather systems firsthand. The thought was chilling to say the least. I am sure Adam and Mike would give me all the information and paint a good picture but I wanted to see it myself. New Zealand was only 500 miles to the West, and I thought about heading back and having a new computer brought out. Then I remembered that Cyclone Gita was due to make landfall there in a few days. I had reached a new low point for the voyage. I was sure if given the opportunity to jump ship and head for land I would have. Once again, my isolation, along with another Cyclone, would be the unpassable barrier that kept me from stopping the voyage.

After a time of wallowing to match the motion of Sparrow, I went to work on trying everything I could to make the backup computer work with the satellite phone. Normally, if Adam tells me something can't be done on a computer then I wouldn't even try. But I had plenty of time on my hands and needed something to occupy me during the abysmal calm we were in. The instructions for configuring the computer to link with the sat phone came with about 20 steps for 3 different operating systems. I just went down the line and tried each one. The first round took me just about two hours and didn't work at all. I then dove into the firewalls and virus protection settings, network setting and Wi-Fi, turning everything off.

I wondered what it would be like to have full satellite technology on this trip. Be able to watch TV and stream movies? Besides costing a fortune, I think more than anything I would have missed out on so much with my eyes glued to a screen. What would be the point of sailing around the world if I was doing it as if from a couch in the living room of a house? I was glad to have only nature as my entertainment. After another hour, and more failed attempts, I took a break and then had an idea.

The computer that I was given as a backup was from my Mother. A much nicer computer than anything I had ever had, all the bells and whistles. Maybe I could make the computer more like Sparrow. Simplify it. I went into every setting I could and turned them all off, restarting each time. After another 2 hours my eyes were starting to get red and lose focus. Another round with the 20 steps, failure again. As if to clear my head, a puff of breeze made its way in the cabin and brought me on deck to find some wind filling in from the South West. The computer would have to wait.

Nothing; and I mean nothing; can compare to the relief that comes with a building wind after hours and hours of bobbing in the open ocean. It could be compared to flying down the freeway with no traffic around. Then you see the brake lights ahead. Then you slow way down. Stop and go for an hour. The next part is a dead stop. Let's just say you then put the car in park and read a sign that says, "Stay in Your Car." Not to mention, your car is lurching up and down and rolling from side to side. 11 hours pass. In that time, you have cleaned every corner of the interior, added to the preset stations on the radio, had lunch and dinner, and maybe fixed some broken part of the car. Now think of how happy you would be if you saw the brake lights come back on and the cars move ahead and the road clears in minutes. That was how I felt getting through yet another calm.

The sails were up in minutes with whoops of joy and relief. Sometimes it felt so good to get the wind back, it almost made the calm worth happening just to feel the high when it is over. Our world was steady again and back on track. Heading East and moving well, it was time to get back to work on the computer.

I was running out of options and ways to tweak any more settings. I had been at this for nearly 6 hours by this point but again, I had all the time in the world. I noticed the bluetooth icon in the corner of the screen. Turned it off. Reset computer. Launch driver, waiting to connect, still waiting, verifying, registering, connected! I held my breath and didn't even want to think that it was actually working, but with cautious fingers I open the weather program, download weather, error, but still connected. Download weather, error, download weather. This went on for about 10 tries, each time I would hit enter and the error would come up; but then it didn't. The computer was thinking, and then I saw it. The little green progress bar moving from left to right and the percentage going up. I froze. After a minute the process was complete and the file was saved. I had the updated weather. Before looking at the update I went on deck to enjoy my moment of triumph! Computers were a mystery to me but I had done it. I couldn't wait to tell Adam about this. The one time in my life I was able to do something computer related that he couldn't! The impossible dream. I didn't want to jinx it so I went below with a big smile, life back on track, and Sparrow sailing. Opening the new weather map, I froze again.

The gentle breeze that was filling Sparrow's sails was due to increase to Gale force, F-8, in 12 hours. That was the good news from what I was seeing on the screen. Cyclone Gita would be arriving in two days' time and looked ugly. A mess of a system that would be falling apart hopefully as it made its way from New Zealand, apparently dead set on finding us! At least I could see it now. I could see into the future and for that I was happy. Unnerved, for sure, but happy I knew what was coming all the same. A check on deck while there was still some light in the sky. I wanted to make sure that as the winds came on in the night, we would be ready. The heavy winds always seemed to build in the night.

The gale rose and fell with its peak around 0600 the next morning. By 0400 the following day we were once again becalmed on a freshly churned up ocean. February 21st brought an Easterly wind and we took advantage to get as far South as possible, running away from the Cyclone to colder waters. Squalls rolled over us as we sailed slowly over a very heavy swell from the South West. The biggest catch so far of 12 gallons of fresh water. As we closed in on 50 degrees South latitude, I felt that we had gone far enough, and for the next 24 hours we Hove-to and I slept.

By noon on February 22nd we had lost 25 miles to the West. The pressure had dropped to an all-time low of 970 as the remnants of Gita calmed the winds and disturbed the seas. We had found our way into the eye of a dying Cyclone. A wave set from the North East and another from the South West were playing with Sparrow as if she was nothing more than a cork. All sail down, the motion was very violent and in multiple directions. Mongo was losing his mind when we would sometimes be shoved astern. I disconnected him and lashed the tiller a midship. Unable to do anything but laugh, I watched the show of waves and listened to sound of breakers all around.

I am not sure how or why the waves were still breaking without the wind, but these waves were falling all over themselves and sometimes right over the bow and stern. There was nothing dangerous about these waves, but every so often I would hear what sounded more like a shore break, off in the distance and well out of sight. Whenever the sea changes it never goes unnoticed. As miserable as the motion was, I couldn't help but be amazed by the sight of the ripple free, rolling sea. Hours fell away and nothing seemed to happen besides the accumulation of clouds all around. They darkened the sky and brought about an early start to the night.

Just as complete darkness fell over us, I was once again shown just how drastic the world changes in the Southern Ocean. As quick as the snap of a finger, the wind came on and came on strong. F-0 to F-9 from the North without any warning. I first tried to get the mainsail up but found the halyards getting too tangled around the mast steps in the driving winds. The staysail was set to help calm the bucking motion and get a little speed under Sparrow's keel.

Uneasy with the walloping gusts and shifting winds, I sailed with just the staysail for the first few hours. Holding just about 5 knots and heading just North of East, I felt like a fly, the waves trying desperately to slap together around us. The waves from the South West would power us up and Sparrow would heel under the push to windward. Then, just as fast, the waves from the North East would steal the wind by shoving us to leeward. No question of getting any sleep until the chaos ended. Thankfully, the North East wave set fell away quickly and throughout the night the world seemed to restore itself to some sort of order.

The winds slowly backed through the night requiring constant adjustments to our heading and sail plan. As the winds dropped to a steady F-7, the 2nd reefed mainsail flew. Heading almost dead downwind we rolled and surfed into the next day. The sun peaked out and the seas wore a cold dark blue as if to say, the further South the darker the ocean. But our heading now was back to the North East. With a bone in her teeth, Sparrow plied the sea back away from the Furious 50's to between the 45-47 degrees South latitude. I had planned to stay there for most of the Pacific crossing; it seemed a safer, albeit longer, route to the Horn.

By midnight on February 24th the winds were howling at F-8 with the occasional squall increasing the screaming wind through the rigging to F-9 or more. With only the 3rd reef in the mainsail and the waves building to an average of 25 feet or so, I wondered just how bad this gale would become. 300 feet of 2-inch-thick line sat idle in the cabin. If needed I could tow it behind with an anchor attached. This, I figured, would help steady Sparrow. I had also pulled out the small storm jib but it sat in the cabin unused.

A common line running in my mind when at sea is, "Better to do it now rather than wait until conditions gets worse." Time to get wet and head out on deck to prepare the storm jib, just in case. Sail bag in hand, I crawled from the cockpit under the spray of the sea, the roar of the waves made more intense by the pitch-black night. No moon or stars to be seen through the shroud of thick clouds. On the foredeck the world seemed a little less violent being in the lee of the mainsail and 30 feet of Sparrow.

Every movement had to be planned and controlled as we dropped down the face of a wave, sped forward, then angled up as the wave passed around us. Each hank took a few seconds but soon the sail was secured to the inner stay and lashed. The sheets and halyard were next. I sat dumbfounded, looking at the jib cars that the sheets were led to. "Where was I supposed to set them? Hole three or was it all the way forward?" I went with hole number three and called it good. A quick double check over the job just completed and it was back to the cockpit.

The dodger was rattling in the increasing winds from astern and it too was lashed down. The difference that made to my world was astounding. Suddenly, there was nothing to hide behind. Sparrow felt small and exposed amongst the ever-breaking waves. Dripping wet, I brought a good amount of the sea with me down below. The cabin was wet almost everywhere. Half the sea and half condensation, I slid the companionway hatch closed and sat in my dark and dingy cave. Pinned into the nav station I took in the scene, every surface either damp or dripping. I used a hand towel to mop up what I could and rung it out in the sink, over and over. Never really drying anything but just getting rid of the puddles. Thankfully, my bunk was about the only place that seemed untouched from drips, damp for sure but no drips to make an excessive wet spot. Though on this night I would have no use for my bunk.

With the peace of mind from having rigged the storm jib and the exhaustion of not sleeping much since the calms of Gita, I took a few salt incrusted cockpit cushions and laid them on the cabin sole. I was going to sleep in my wet weather gear for the night. At first, I didn't think sleep would be possible under the relentless noise of the wind and the vibrations as Sparrow surfed the waves. But in minutes I was out, Mongo at the helm and

Sparrow riding out another gale just as she was designed to do, and by this point I think because she liked to as well.

Chapter 35
Ships Log

2200 April 9th, 2018
Lat 54 46'S, Long 062 17'W
Days at Sea: 190

Wild drop in the Pressure over the last 24 hours. The wind and sea are heavy and changing, the currents are all over place running around the small islands in the area. Sparrow is doing her best just to keep bashing through it all.

Conditions are just getting worse and worse. We took a huge hit from a random wave filling the cockpit and pouring into the engine room. My poor engine. Winds have veered to the North, so we are just trying to hold our position, but it is tough going. The motion of the boat is pretty awful. So, no projects for now and the engine will have to wait. Battery power is below 10V, for all purposes the batteries are dead. Not good. I am sure my world could be worse, I could still be West of the Horn after all, but I could really use a break from the cold, fog, and wild moody winds.

Becalmed as night begins to fall and we are drifting on the slightest breeze, just glad the seas have eased as well so still making some way to the East North East. Time to get working on the engine fuel system.

Shoot! I broke the glass under the fuel filter. Any hope of having the safety net of an engine for getting into Port Stanley is gone. Now my nerves are at an end. Maybe I can get a replacement in the Falkland's but I really just wanted to have the engine for the Falkland's! I hate being so close to land with no engine. Going to have to stay on my toes. My seamanship is getting another test. Not in a good mental state tonight, sleep is going to be hard with all the thoughts of impending problems that could arise in the coming days.

Chapter 36
At Nature's Whim

Sparrow really does enjoy heavy weather and it would always show in the daily miles. Since the awful calm of Gita, we had made nearly 450 miles in three days! Like always, the winds were never consistent like in the trades. By March 1st we were once again rolling in the aftermath of such a strong wind. The weather forecast showed a mess of small systems both North and South but more worrisome were the calm patches in between. Just when the miles were really adding up, we were getting hit by an Easterly speed bump.

As the winds swung around to the East South East, I had to make a choice. Head due North and risk running into a large calm. Plus, sail past the 45 degrees South latitude that I wanted to stay at or below. The other option was to head to the South South West and stay closer to the heavy winds. The second option would mean beating hard into both wind and sea to try to lose as little ground as possible. I chose the Southern route.

-March 1st, 2018 Journal:
A day of despair. I miss everything I left ashore. The wind is hard to deal with, we pound endlessly. I hate looking at the chart. Just want to head East and make miles.-

One of the shortest daily journal entries of the trip. Above the gales and the calms, nothing was more disheartening than losing ground and taking a beating while doing so. When the pounding became too much, we would take a break and go Hove-to for a while. It seemed as though just as I had a sail plan that was working, Mother Nature would change her mind and I would be back on deck to try something else. I was glad, however, to have the work to help pass the time.

We were looking at three days of these conditions before the winds would allow our heading to continue to the East. Truly, we were at Nature's Whim. A thought kept running through my head during this time. The owner of the Bitter End Yacht Club, Richard, told me the night before I departed that, "no matter what is going on or how bad things seem, the winds will always change." What I gleaned from his statement was that even though I don't know when the wind will change, all I had to do was keep going until it does. It may seem a very obvious notion, but when alone and facing a world that seems dead set on stopping one from pushing forward, having a finish line is very important. No matter if that line is a day or a month away, or in this case an imaginary wind line that I hoped would come sooner rather than later. Just like the calm after the storm, I could count on the winds eventually changing.

As the winds did eventually come around from the South, light and variable, our heading changed back to almost due East. And just in time; on March 3rd we had made only 40 miles in 24 hours but mostly in the wrong direction! The forecast looked good for the following week with a long run of North and North West winds. If this held true, we would make up for the last two weeks of terrible sailing. Looking back along the chart of the Pacific was very discouraging. We had barely moved as we sailed South from New Zealand. Then running from Gita followed by the Easterly winds. Like a giant "S curve" instead of a nice straight line, if this continued, we would be lucky to make the Horn by the end of April and well past summer.

We were in a race against time. The short amount of time to get out of the Southern Ocean before winter set in, the time left that Sparrow and I could endure the punishment, and the time when the food would run out. We had been at sea for 150 days and sailed some 17,000 miles. All that was behind us as we crept slowly out into the largest expanse of open ocean on the planet.

Chapter 37
Ships Log

2100 April 10th, 2018
Lat 54 34'S, Long 060 43'W
Days at Sea: 191

    Had a little sun today and did a system check with the bilge pumps, glad to have the power but found the pump is not working. I replaced the pump and still no luck, investigated the hose and the last 5 feet of hose have broken free and formed a dip in the line that has created some kind of air lock. That fixed, everything works great. I never had to change the pump in the first place! I hate it when I do that. After all this time I should know to start with the easy stuff while working any problem.

    Winds have backed to the West! Heading right for the mark now and feeling good. My emotions are riding a roller coaster at this point. With the winds ever changing and the fact that I have to get close to land I am definitely stressed. Only two days until I have food again, the silver lining.

    After a quick ETA check I have to slow up a bit. If the forecast holds true, I could be arriving in the middle of the night. No way I am going to try to attempt that, not with the winds and squalls increasing by the minute. In a day I will be sailing just off the Eastern shore of the Falkland's which should cut the waves and make life a bit more comfortable. The trade is that I will get no sleep at all. As great as Mongo has done, if the winds shift and I am dead asleep, we could end up on the rocks faster than I want to think.

Got to see just a sliver of a sunset tonight, normally nothing new but I have not seen that in many weeks. My spirits are high right now, I am heading just East of North and things are already warming up! The seas are not so bad, so projects continue. I was able to get up the mast to inspect the holes for the VHF antenna but that is all. The actual repair will have to wait for another day.

Not a bad day at all, 2 gallons of water caught, projects underway, sunset and even the stars came out. It was a little too cold for a long star gazing session but a good reminder of what lies ahead and thus pushes me to get North. Soon I will be surrounded by sun, warmth and star filled nights.

Chapter 38
Dwindling Supplies

The first week in March put us still over 3,000 miles from Cape Horn. With winds as steady as we had seen so far in the Pacific, the miles were adding up once again. Warmer air coming from the North and hitting the cold Southern Ocean was producing thick fog and shrouding our world in a dull light by day and a pitch-black void by night. However, the seas were relatively calm and I used the time to take account of my food stores and supplies.

A normal day of dining aboard Mighty Sparrow was becoming bleak at best. In the morning I would have 1 cup of oatmeal with a dollop of maple syrup for flavor. All the bags of dried fruit were long gone and thoughts of greasy omelets, bacon and potatoes filled my head. In two minutes, breakfast would be over but the hunger always stayed.

By noon I could have a lite lunch of 1 ½ cups of dehydrated rice or noodles. Because this had to be cooked, I was able to enjoy every second from the smell of the steaming food while holding the warm cup in my hand. Each bite was a blast of flavor! And that is really saying something when eating "Chicken flavored Rice Dish." If I was working hard, I would have a can of vegetables or fruit just to keep my energy up and help fill the void in my stomach. Never once did I miss glancing over at the remaining food stores to think about diving in for another round.

Dinner was the big treat. An MRE entrée, full of flavor and as hot as I could make it. The hotter it is the slower I would eat it. Generally, I would just cut the corner from the bag and suck out the contents. Spaghetti, Ravioli, RSPP, these were all long gone. I was down to chicken stew and a few potato sides. A few bags of rice and lentils added a bit of weight to the meal if I was again working hard for the day. But in the current conditions sailing was easy and so eating was light. If I could sleep through a meal it was a win, if I couldn't help myself and I ate a double helping of oatmeal it was a win/loss. A win by the energy it gave me but a loss as I had just stolen from the future me.

It seemed that every few days I would pull every plastic container out and condense the food stores, always counting and making lists. I would go through the empty compartments that once were packed so tightly with food that I couldn't open the doors without bags of stores fall out. I found myself checking over and over, looking for the hidden gem. Adam had stashed a few snacks and bags of candy around Sparrow the day before I departed. Unfortunately, I had found most of them in the first few days. But the thought that there might be a candy bar lurking somewhere was enough to send me into a complete search over every cabinet. One day I even went into the emergency grab bag to see if I had long ago put some supplies in there, and what a surprise! 14 MRE entrees! And not the old Chicken Stew either; spaghetti and ravioli! I guess I was figuring I wanted to have the good stuff if I was going to be in the life raft!

Hunger is something that I luckily have only had to dabble with in my life. I was fortunate to have parents who worked very hard to make sure there was not only food on the table, but good food as well. Besides a few poorly provisioned camping trips, and by that, I mean I ate too much too fast and ran out, my only prolonged experience with true hunger was on the Appalachian Trail. That hunger comes from the excessive work of hiking 10-12 hours a day. Even though I was eating almost 5,000 calories a day, an AT hiker is never satisfied!

What I was experiencing as we sailed deeper into the Pacific was a hunger from a lack of food alone. I would wake up with a pit in my stomach and the sounds that go along with it. I spent each day dreaming of food that was over a thousand miles away in any direction. I went to bed hungry. Even as I ate, I was hungry. Sometimes it felt that my stomach complained more after I had just eaten than before. It is a truly miserable state to be in and I had a long time to go before anything could be done about it.

For me, it was a big realization about the state of our world. At 39 years old this was the first time I did not have enough food to eat. For so many people all over the world, hunger is a fact they can't escape from. I thought of people begging for money in big cities whom I had passed right by without much thought. I wondered whether maybe they feel the same hunger as I was feeling now. I would certainly help a hungry person and get them some food. The insight I was getting into this world of suffering was about the only bright side of my situation.

Along with the food stores, spare parts were starting to be used more and more. Two of the jib car blocks had begun to crack with corrosion and needed to be replaced. Another block for the staysail halyard was replaced as the bearings had been worn down from the constant pressure. With each broken part removed and replaced, it was one less quick and easy repair that I could do. Halyards chafed and were shortened. Sails were taken down and the sewing machine came out to mend them. On the whole, Sparrow was holding together very well I thought. No big breaks and nothing so far that couldn't be fixed with the parts and tools that we had on board.

After 4 great days of sailing in endless fog and steady North winds, I was at the Nav station filling in the log and eyeing a can of pears I had promised to wait until dinner to eat. And then a loud bang! Followed instantly by the flogging of a sail, untethered in the wind. On deck in a second, I looked forward to see the staysail flying to leeward and violently shaking the rig. The staysail stay had broken and everything was chaos in the F-4 to 5 winds. Quickly I released the halyard and the sail eased but didn't drop more than a foot. I jumped forward and grabbed the lazy sheet, wanting to keep some distance from the heavy steal turnbuckle that was whipping around at the bottom of the sail. One hit from that solid piece of steel would have been really bad. The sail came down half way then stopped. The halyard had fouled and back to the cockpit I went. The halyard free to run I went forward again and continued to wrestle with the flogging sail. Once the sail was on the deck and out of the wind the whole world seemed to go quiet once again.

Upon inspection it was not the stay that had broken, but the large eyebolt that was its anchor point. Most likely part of the original build, the eyebolt was over 40 years old and had sheared off where the nut was located and had been for decades. Lashing everything in place and setting the #3 jib, I changed Sparrow's heading to a broad reach to take the pressure off the mast. It was time to take a long look at the damage done and the possible ways to remedy the situation. One of the many lessons that I had learned from reading old sailing books was to always think through any repairs long before going into action. Like the old sailors, I wanted to fix this only once and do a damn good job of it. There was still Cape Horn to round after all!

Chapter 39
Ships Log

1800 April 11th, 2018
Lat 53 04'S, Long 058 52'W
Days at Sea: 192

Huge Squall got me on deck very early. Skipped the 2nd reef and went right to 3rd reef and storm jib. Beating hard into the wind but barely making any headway. The small sails and the blanket of barnacles on the boat are not helping Sparrow sail like she wants to. I am hoping the seas will ease up as we close the distance to the islands. Ha, I hope for a lot of things these days it seems.

Rice for breakfast, again. Squalls for lunch, and rice again for dinner! This is Cape Horn Sailing! I often think of what life was like for those sailors on their tall ships, flying round the Horn. I wonder what they would think of my little boat, probably call me a damn fool!

Squalls are becoming more and more violent now. Every 30 minutes or so another rolls over us. Down to 3rd Reef Main only and just about running with the wind. Lots of hail and snow. On the foredeck changing out the storm jib when a bad one came through; my hands are bleeding from the ice. Nothing I could do but protect my eyes. I am keeping my ski goggles on my head for the night.

Looking like I should see the light house outside of Port Stanley around 6 am, perfect! I have no engine, VHF, or detailed chart of the area. So, this will be a real adventure! I have been given a rough picture of what to expect but I must say I really wish I would have brought a chart for the Falkland Islands. Seems like a big oversight on my part.

Chapter 40
Into the Abyss

As a broken Sparrow sailed its half-starved and half crazed crew deeper and deeper into the empty Pacific, the fog became so overwhelming that the normal world seemed a distant memory. The winds calmed on March 12th and the plan for fixing the stay was put into action.

Though the spectra line I had used to lash the stay into place seemed very strong, I wanted steel to be the anchor point. None of the spare eyebolts were of the right size but I had enough stainless steel and threaded rod to make a very strong replacement. But the idea that I had come up with would be much simpler than that, if it worked. As the original eyebolt had sheared off where the nut was, I only needed to dig away at the bowsprit far enough to sink the bolt in about half an inch to expose enough threads to get a new nut and washer on.

After inspecting the old eyebolt for any signs of other cracks or weak points, it seemed in great shape. Most likely some corrosion was to blame between the nut and the threads. A little Teflon gel would solve that by protecting the metal from further corrosion. Grinding away with the Dremel, I was glad to see that the wood was still hard and dry and showed no signs of rot. Back and forth between digging and placing the eyebolt to see if I was deep enough, the whole time bobbing up and down and keeping an eye out for a wave that would like to jump aboard and soak my tools and me.

After about an hour, I had the eyebolt firmly in place and covered with 5200 sealant to keep the sea out of the fresh wood of the bow sprit. Once the Stay was attached everything looked as though nothing had ever happened. But knowing that it did happen, and that the eyebolt was so old, I added a good lashing of Spectra line to make sure that if it did happen again, I would have some time to get the sail down and not have to wrestle it like before. I was lucky that it had happened in the relatively calm conditions and wind. I wondered what it would have been like to deal with the same problem in a F-9 gale!

With Sparrow back in shape I was able to concentrate on a few other issues that were becoming more and more apparent. The first was the colony of gooseneck barnacles that had hitched a ride below the water line. I had first noticed them near the equator when there was only one or two. Like rabbits they multiplied very rapidly. I could only see that they had covered the entire rudder, and I expected that the rest of Sparrow's hull was the same. I didn't think it was really affecting the speed in the heavy winds and seas but as the winds became light, I could tell they were adding quite a bit of drag and something needed to be done.

Now, it seems a simple idea to just jump overboard with a scraper and swim around freeing the little goosenecks and whistling while you do it. Not so. The first problem is the temperature of the water. Very cold doesn't do justice to what it felt like when I put my hand into the sea. The bigger problem was that the never-ending rolling of Sparrow would make any job under the water very difficult. But the thing that was keeping me on deck and looking for another solution was that I was just outright scared to swim in the Southern Ocean.

So far on the voyage we had encountered many whales, dolphins, and even a few small sharks. At night I would see endless eyes shining back under the light of my headlamp. There were things down there so big I wouldn't be more than a snack. The more I thought about what lies beneath, the less I was going to just jump right in and start making noise, as well as send a trail of barnacles twinkling into the deep. Creatures would follow that trail for sure! So, I opted for the next best thing.

I first screwed the large paint scraper to a 4-foot broom handle. With this I dangled as far as I could over the side of Sparrow's deck and was able to reach almost the entire rudder. The Goosenecks came off from the antifouling paint easily. The ones that had made their way up past the waterline were a bit more difficult and I didn't want to attack them with too much vigor as Sparrow is a beautiful boat and I wanted to keep her that way. Scratching her paint to get rid of a few barnacles didn't seem worth it, and quite frankly a bit disrespectful to my partner which had seen me through so many miles around the planet.

As I couldn't reach very far below the waterline around the rest of the hull, I added another few feet of pipe to the brush handle. A little rickety and looking like some taped together crane, I was getting far below the water line and the trail of Goosenecks fell away. A few hours of this and I had made my way around the hull and called the job done. Without being able to inspect my work I wasn't really sure it was worth the trouble, but plenty of the little stowaways were gone and sometimes just a little effort is great for morale.

With the light foggy winds dropping, our daily miles fell below 100. Even though we were nearing the absolute middle of the South Pacific, Point Nemo, the fog kept our world closed in with only the occasional peak of blue sky. Days passed and always the fog stayed. The waves would come up and down from different directions as low-pressure systems passed to the South and North. Sparrow's motion, ever changing, kept me working constantly with the sails to keep us going. We were in limbo. Every day seemed the same, nothing to see but fog and the waves that appeared and disappeared from the void. This was about the time that I started to notice the mold.

I had become very used to the damp conditions in the cabin. Most nights I could see my own breath condensing on the non-insulated fiberglass as well as the bronze portholes. When we entered the fog, we were now essentially a moving sponge, soaking up all the moisture the air could give us. I first saw the little black specs on the white walls. Soon the constantly damp charts were producing a black tint on the edges. Then my pillow, a dark red camping pillow, seemed decidedly darker in color. Upon closer inspection I could see that a good sized colony of mold had sprung up. I had been pressing my face against it every night! The only thing that had been spared from the outbreak was me; I examined my beard and all was well. I had few options to deal with the problem.

The charts, I would continue to dry out over the stove, very carefully holding each one until the crisp feel of dry paper was returned. As for the pillow? I put a dry tee shirt over it and then a seemingly mold free pillow case over that. I had one bottle of an all-purpose cleaner but I wasn't going to use that until things warmed up and I was out of the Southern Ocean. I figured I could live with the current situation for the next month. I never considered it could be bad for my health, so I let the mold enjoy its time aboard Mighty Sparrow. We were becoming an ecosystem.

A near gale sprung up from the East North East on March 14th. All we could do was sit Hove-to and wait until things changed. And change the wind did. All day the sails went up and down. We were becalmed, then beaten by the near gale and then bashed by waves and then becalmed again. By the end of the day I was exhausted.

List of Sail Changes from 0600-1700 March 14th

1st Reef Main/ Staysail

2nd Reef Main/ Staysail

3rd Reef Main/ Staysail

Hove to with Storm sails

3rd Reef Main/ Storm Jib

2nd Reef Main/ Storm Jib

2nd Reef Main/ Staysail

1st Reef Main/ Staysail

1st Reef Main/ Staysail/ #2 Jib

Full Main/ Staysail

Full Main/ Staysail/#3 Jib

All sails down/ Becalmed

Each sail change required getting back into my wet weather gear, then going on deck and getting soaked. It would only take few minutes to change the sails then down below I would go. Never more than an hour would pass before heading back on deck and doing another sail change. Each time I shipped a good amount of salt water down below to add to the damp conditions of the cabin. With all the work, the day came to an end quickly in a windless and foggy world. We had covered just 50 miles in 24 hours. At first, I was discouraged by the low miles, but soon I realized that those were my miles. I had put in the effort to keep Sparrow moving that day and I was proud of what I had done. Sleep came fast after a quick meal with the addition of a can of corn as my reward. However slowly, we were still making miles.

The conditions deteriorated to a miserable state for days. Winds ever changing and dropping to nothing almost each day at least once. With every change in direction, the waves were built up and now came from the North, South, and East. When the winds came from the East, I found that our tacking angle was about 180 degrees. I had to laugh at this point. With the waves so confused and the barnacles slowing us down we were no longer able to sail to windward. Not even one degree!

-March 18th 2018 Journal:

Let me paint a picture of this fine Southern Ocean morning. The stove is burning away to add a little heat to the 38-degree air in the cabin. I have pinned myself into the Nav station as Sparrow lurches up and down 10 feet with every wave from the East and the South. The wind is switching between East and North East every ten minutes. Our heading changes accordingly from 180 to 110 degrees on the compass. The wind force changes as well. So not only do we lurch up and over each wave but now we heel over to 30 degrees in the puffs and then lie flat in the lulls. My shoulder is killing me so I took one of the strong pain killers from the med kit. Feeling good and laughing out loud. The conditions are so bad it has become a comedy or maybe a tragedy, not sure.-

I have always had the ability to laugh at some of the worst situations that I get myself into. Long before my solo adventures I remember a time when I had set up my camping tarp in a seemingly great spot for the night. Sometime around 3 am, the rains came and low and behold I hadn't found a great spot at all; I was sleeping in a hole! As the icy cold water started to seep into my sleeping bag I woke. The foam pad I was sleeping on had become an island. The rain continued and soon I found myself sitting in about 3 inches of water. There was nothing I could do; the sleeping bag was wet but warm from my body heat. All I could do was sit there and wait for morning. Incredibly, I started to laugh. Giggling at first, and then almost uncontrollably laughing when the rain fell harder and harder. To be able to laugh at the worst of times was a great help during my voyage midway across the Pacific.

The beating continued, but by March 20th we were as close to Point Nemo as we would get. Sparrow was sailing about 25 miles North of the furthest point from land anywhere on the planet! Over 8 million square miles of empty ocean and we were a dot in the middle. For me this was a special time, and although the flags didn't come out on this day, I did send a bit of Buzz over the side thinking that this was a place he would have loved to have been. Although there was nothing different to look at, I had a sense of reaching a mountaintop. Instead of getting further from land we were now getting closer.

The day did bring a sad truth about our world. I had spent most of the day on deck in awe of my position at the end of the earth. During that time, I was still able to see a plastic bottle floating on the surface. A very common sight in many places in our oceans. But way out at the farthest reaches? I didn't expect to see it and soon realized that we have polluted every mile of our ocean world. Not one place is free from the plague of single use plastic trash. Not one single place.

Chapter 41
Ships Log

2300 April 12th, 2018
Lat 51 24'S, Long 057 38'W
Days at Sea: 193

A sleepless stressful night to say the least. Running a few miles off the East coast of the Falkland Islands, squalls rolled over us all night. The seas are kind but the winds are jumping from F-6 to F-8. It would have been nice to see these storied islands as I sail past but I am just so glad I don't have to push to get to Port Stanley.

Lights in the distance keep me checking my heading to stay in the clear of the few rocks that lie off shore on my approach. No sleep as I go from the nav station to the cockpit, over and over through the night. I must push through for a few more hours and then I will be sailing North East and away from the dangers of land.

At last, the blinking of a lighthouse! Just as the half-light filled the sky, I have made the mark and just have to get into the bay. The image I have in my mind of what I should see is completely different from what I am seeing now. I was told about three islands just inside the bay past the light house. I see three rock islands just offshore from the point where the lighthouse sits.

What I wouldn't give for a chart of the Falkland's!

My heading is fine but to enter the bay from my position I will cut in-between the islands. The South swell is my savior, there is no indication of shallow water between the rocks. If I go around it will take an extra hour but if I go for the cut I will be in the bay in minutes. At the last minute I bear away and take one long hard look with the binoculars and decide to just go for it. Normally, I would have never taken the chance but after no sleep for 24 hours I think I just wanted to get this over with.

With a nervous hand ready to jibe if a closer look shows shallow water, we plunged forward and pass through the gap and into the bay. The winds are howling, whales and seals are around, and I scan the bay for hazards. What a sight! The mountains disappearing behind the hail squalls. Down to storm sails, Sparrow strains to get up wind. We have about a mile on each tack and try to stay as far from danger as possible. Without the engine we could get into trouble fast.

A text comes in from Jim. I have been spotted and the boat should be on the way soon. "Look for the red powerboat." I realize that even though I am alone here in Port Stanley, lots of people are going to be wondering just how this operation is going. I can feel their eyes on me. I also feel a little uneasy to see and talk to other people. I wonder what they will think of me and my food drop? I wonder if they will be mad that they had to come out here in this nasty weather.

After two hours of tacking back and forth I see the boat, bright red and about 35 feet long. They come right over with big smiles and cameras pointed right at me. After a few pleasantries they point me to a little bay a mile up wind. Sparrow and I try to get moving, the going is very slow up wind. I hand the Storm Jib and replace it with the Staysail. Now we're getting somewhere.

Slowly but surely the wave chop stops and they pull alongside. No lines, just a handshake and the boxes start flying. 30 hours of stress to get in here and in 2 minutes the job is done. I told them I was so glad they came out in this weather and they tell me of the weather coming in. I know the forecast but a little local knowledge is never a bad thing.

They watch over me as I drift, bare poles, out of the bay while I stow as much as I can. But first and for most, I grab the bottle of Scotch, a toast to the guys, to the Falkland's, and to Neptune for allowing all this to happen. Of course, after a double for me!

No time to waste and I set the 3rd reef in the mainsail and start my way North East. Ships around and I have too much to do all at once. The food needs to be unpacked and cardboard needs to go! So much packing tape makes for a bit of work to clean the boxes before they can go overboard and into the sea to safely biodegrade. I toss the pieces in the cockpit for now. Wind and seas are increasing, squalls continue to hit us, but Sparrow holds her own and I switch between madly eating cookies, shipping the cardboard and stowing food wherever I can. No longer concerned where it goes, just pack it safe for now and planning to repack it all later when the weather calms down.

A big wave jumped aboard and filled the cockpit. We are getting pummeled out here. In the squalls we have enough sail but when they pass the waves are getting into the cockpit. The boat feels wrong. A look on deck and the sea is everywhere! 6 inches on the deck and I see the problem, the scuppers are clogged with wet cardboard. No time for safety I got on deck and over it all went. I clear the scuppers and immediately Sparrow reacts to the lightened load.

As the sun sets I have almost everything stowed with the exception of a few items that I continue to devour with cries of joy at each bite. After many attempts we have a new forecast and another 6 hours or so of this heavy weather. Winds are up to F-9 with hail and snow. The squalls are easing up a bit but the hatches are still covered with slush. The cabin is very wet and must be mopped up every few hours.

I make the first cup of coffee I have had in over a month, absolutely the best drink of my life! The fridge is running with 12.2 volts on the batteries, I hope they hold. Precious food in there now! Dinner tonight is a simple ham sandwich, too rough to cook but no matter as I have been dreaming of fresh bread since I left Gloucester.

My clothes are wet, body is beat up and muscles sore from all the work to get to the food drop. No sleep for almost 40 hours and I'm exhausted. Off to my bunk to try to get some sleep on a rolling windy night. Nope! The AIS alarm is ringing out not 5 minutes after getting in the sleeping bag.

A ship 6 miles out on the same heading but steaming at twice the speed. My heading is swinging over 45 degrees as the waves and swell push us around and we surf wildly to the North East. I try to get them on the VHF but nothing comes back. They are within a mile now and I can see their lights between the waves, still no answer to my calls. I break out the handheld radio from the emergency grab bag and call on that, nothing still. I don't know why I even try. Gone are the days of ships hailing each other out of respect or even safety.

I put more North in my heading but that brings the waves on the beam and we take a few big hits. Only a little more Sparrow, just hang in there. As soon as I know we are safe I return to running in the seas and the ship disappears into the night. I am sure there was never a real risk of collision but my nerves are shattered. At the very least I know the AIS is working and that will make sleeping much better. Off to my bunk just before midnight, Sparrow carries me once more through the storm and I trust she will not let me down.

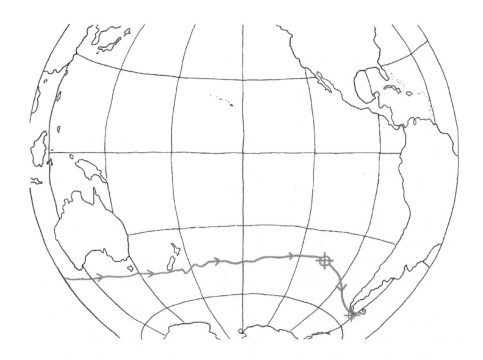

Chapter 42
Approaching the 5th Cape

     As much as the wind and waves dictated our heading, it was time to start the approach to Cape Horn. Leaving 120 degrees West longitude in our wake, it would not be long before we started to put some South into our heading. I was becoming more worried each day as the weather forecast showed gale after gale running to the Horn, right where we were heading. The winds were growing stronger and seas more confused. They tossed Mighty Sparrow around worse than ever.

     With the temperature dropping into the 30's my world below deck became even more damp and disgusting. Any time I needed to mark a chart it had to be dried over the stove first or the pencil would just tear right through. The only way I could keep at all warm was to be wearing every piece of clothing that wasn't completely soaked. I had made the mistake of going forward for a quick check of the staysail stay when a random wave caught me and soaked through a few layers, and worse yet, the sweater my Mother made for me! To fend off the cold I wore 6 layers on top and three on the bottom, two pairs of socks, a neck warmer and winter hat. Any time I needed to be on deck, I added two layers of wet weather pants and one of the two jackets depending on which was less soaked. I couldn't remember the last time I had felt warm and it was going to get much worse before it got better.

Breaking my own rules, I would let my mind wander ahead into the Atlantic Ocean and the warm sun that I would find there. I couldn't wait to get out of the Southern Ocean. This harsh world had been wearing on Sparrow and me for far too long now. I wished for nothing more than to get out and the last thing I wanted to do was to sail further South into colder more violent weather. I had many thoughts of abandoning the trip at this point.

My eyes looked to the North on the chart where the South Pacific Islands of Tahiti and the Tuamotus spread out. Warm air, calm seas and fresh food. All the things that I have been missing could be had there. Could I ever have lived with the decision to quit? I thought about what that sail would be like mentally. Every minute we sailed North, I would have been questioning if I had made the right choice. I am sure it would have driven me crazy not just for the weeks of sailing but for the rest of my life. Another thought that kept me on track was of the school classrooms that were following the trip. I knew of 4 that were getting my position updates almost every day. I wanted to be able to go and speak to them and tell the story of my voyage. The opportunity to become a real inspiration to people was like a red-hot poker nudging me forward. Sparrow just kept sailing, I was the one questioning what to do.

By the morning of March 23rd, the pressure had dropped

over 24 bars in 24 hours. We were in for yet another gale. By noon the winds were at F-6 from the North West and we ran off to the East South East under the 2nd reefed mainsail. The wind shifted to West South West and brought with it very angry squalls. Some blowing for over an hour at F-10. Down came the mainsail and we were left sailing under the storm jib alone, surfing in the pelting hail. I was glad to see how well Sparrow could do in such strong wind, the strongest so far. I would stand, looking out of the plexiglass in the companion way, grinding my teeth and waiting for something to break. Without the mainsail we seemed to hold our downwind heading much better in the heavy winds. Before, with the 3rd reef pushing us along if the winds rose from a squall, we would sometimes lose our track and end up almost beam to the sea. I would then need to get to the tiller as fast as possible to correct our heading and off we would go. But with just the little scrap of sail, sheeted to the center, the pressure of the screaming winds on the mast were pushing us along. The storm jib did its job and kept Sparrow's bow pointed downwind and running with the tremendous seas.

I couldn't imagine having to go completely bare poles, but I am sure the winds could increase to that point. My plan, if the storm jib was too much sail, was to tow the warp with an anchor from the stern in the hope it would keep us from ending up beam to the seas. I just prayed we wouldn't have to test that plan.

By the next morning the squalls had eased and the winds held from the West South West at F-7. The pressure had jumped back up almost 18 bars but had started to fall off again soon after sunset. Life was miserable and cold. Every time I went on deck, I brought half the ocean back into the cabin. I had found a dry selection of tank top shirts and used them to mop up the now pooling salt water from seemingly everywhere in the cabin. My routine was becoming so basic and repetitive at this point.

Day and night, I would change sails. The food I was eating was always the same. Oatmeal in the morning, dehydrated lunch, and rice with chicken for dinner. Soon I would run out of chicken and only rice with soy sauce would have to suffice. I mopped up the pooling water and held on to every surface whenever I moved. The pressure dropped again and by 0300 on March 27th the winds were back up to gale force. The moon had come out at points during the night and illuminated the angry ocean. Standing at the mast after a sail change, the world was so intense. The waves had grown in height and weight. The sounds of the big breakers would snap my head in their direction. Always a shock at how I could hear them over the sound of the wind in the rigging. We were in the beginning of a very large low-pressure system. It was going to be a long few days.

By noon the winds were at F-9 and the average wave height was around 30 feet. The world was frightening and showing its power. The mainsail was lashed down and again we sailed under the tiny storm jib sheeted home. The pressure started a bit of a rise but the seas kept building and breaking with more strength than before. We were pooped a few times. This is when a massive breaking wave crashes into the cockpit. The pressure of solid water on the washboards in the companion way causes the sea to spray into the cabin like a high-pressure garden hose! Even my bunk was not spared. Out came the tank tops and then some tape to help arrest the water from coming in. A fruitless effort but at least I was trying to help the situation.

An hour after sunset the winds had begun to ease up and were only blowing at F-8. The seas, however, were as big as ever and crossing from the South West and the North West. The first big hit came from the North. Slamming Sparrow's port side hard and direct, this was just a warning shot. On deck all was well but with the winds easing more I had planned to get a little more sail up.

Standing once again at the mast I looked awestruck at the world around me. The moonlit sea was an image I will never forget. The large, breaking white crests thundered around us. We tried to surf but mostly just moved with the waves up and over as they raced under Sparrow's keel. I un-cleated the main halyard and had my arm yanked, almost losing my grip on the line. "What the hell am I doing here?" I had to be the only idiot sailing alone through this storm and trying to put more sail up! But I was trying to give Sparrow the speed she wanted to keep ahead of the breaking waves. It had to be done.

After many tries to free the main halyard from the mast steps and add some sail, I reluctantly gave up until the winds eased a bit more. Things seemed to be ok at the time and I headed down below to my bunk in hopes of forgetting what was going on outside of my little wet cabin. Below I could only hear the passing waves and guess at their size. Not an hour went by before a very large wave came up from the South. It hit us dead on the beam with a force unknown to me until this point. Sparrow yielded and went over in seconds. Looking up at the Stowage closet hanging above me I had a flash of my friend Bob and me screwing the wood together. It held fast but all of the navigation equipment, log books, and various other tools shifted from the nav station to the galley with an amazing clatter. This was all trumped by a loud bang on deck that accompanied the initial hit of the wave. Moving from my bunk to the companionway as Sparrow slowly rolled upright, I was terrified at what I might find.

The dodger had been ripped apart and broken free from one of its anchor points. Luckily it still lay jammed in the cockpit. The spray skirt on the Starboard side had been blown out but everything else seemed to make it through. Back down below and wet weather gear on, I headed back on deck, for I knew then that we absolutely needed more sail up to keep ahead of the waves. I lashed the dodger quickly and then headed back to the mast. A fight that took 45 minutes ensued. Up the mainsail went an inch at a time. I needed to keep Sparrow heading down wind and with the waves. Not an easy point of sail to raise the 3rd reefed mainsail. But little by little I was winning. Another hit came from the North this time and nearly launched me right over the side. Without a second thought I kept at the mainsail and held on tighter.

Once the mainsail came up the storm jib came down. We raced down the waves with a new vigor all together. Sparrow was much happier with the added speed, and so was I. Lashing the dodger with more line for the rest of the night, I said farewell to the outside world and headed down below.

Immediately, I stepped on books, charts, and a million other things that were once secure in the Nav station and now lay in a puddle of salt water on the cabin sole. Collecting them with a quick once over with a wet shirt I stowed them back from where they came. It was a long night of sitting at the Nav station, with the sound of the wave that found us reverberating inside my head. I was unaware at the time, but during the night Sparrow and I had passed the 20,000-mile point on our voyage. We were now 179 days at sea.

Chapter 43
A New Beginning

By 0400 the gale that swept us away from the Falkland Islands began to die off. Once again, the sails came out one reef at a time. As the glow of the coming sun lit the sky we were under full white canvas and still moving well. With a big smile I reached into the fridge and groped around for the eggs. It had been so long since I had a hearty breakfast. With the washing machine motion in the rolling sea, I watched as the eggs scrambled themselves in the pan. My mouth watering like never before, I added cheese and ham. Everything put together onto fresh white bread and toasted. What followed was a breakfast sandwich that I would never, ever, forget. Each bite better than the last, the taste sensations exploded on my tongue. Always a big breakfast guy, for those ten minutes my world had shrunk down to nothing more than each bite going into my mouth.

With breakfast over far too quickly it was time to get to work. This gift of a calm was not going to last and Sparrow was in need of some well-deserved TLC. For the last few weeks I had just been holding on and hoping we would make it as unessential systems broke down. The engine needed to have its fuel system bled and at least given one attempt to start. The VHF aerial was still just hanging in the rigging and everything that was wet down below needed to come up into the sun for the first time in months! Not to mention that I was in need of a good grooming and shower. It had been exactly 2 months since my body felt fresh water.

The VHF was at the top of the list, as I had felt very helpless during the gale by not being able to communicate with the ship. It was also going to be a tough fix and require a few trips up and down the mast. Upon inspection, the antenna was just threaded into the aluminum spreader and corrosion took its toll. I was surprised it stayed in place as long as it had. My plan was to through-bolt the stand in place and make it as solid as possible.

To do such a project in a rolling sea I would need both hands to use the drill and other tools. I put together a short tether for the bosun's chair that I could hook around the mast. The antenna was mounted about 3 feet out on the spreader, which was about 20 feet above Sparrow's deck. I would have to climb to the spreader and hold on with one hand while I clipped the tether around the mast. Once secure, I would carefully remove whichever tool I was using and do the project in steps. Up the mast I went to retrieve the antenna and back down. Up I went with the drill, fighting hard to make three clean holes, and back down. Up I went with the antenna base, and reaching with all my might, pushed all three bolts through and added nuts, and back down. Up I went with the screw driver and wrench. It took a long time to get the base securely in place with the bolts while desperately trying to hold myself steady against the swinging mast. Straining with my feet on one of the mast steps, I felt and heard a pop; one of the rivets had gone! And back down I went. Up with the antenna to connect the cable and hand tighten it to the base, down I went. Up I went with another wrench to make sure the antenna was extra tight, and back down I went. The final trip up was to tape everything to prevent any chafe on the sails, and back down I went, one last time. With muscles physically twitching and shaking I looked at the job with relief and pride. I had no idea if it worked, as no ships were anywhere around, but it looked good and felt solid.

Next up was to pull out as many wet cushions and clothes as I could fit around the deck and life lines to dry in the sun. The air temperature was 58 degrees but the sun felt hot. Even if my clothes don't dry it was good just to give them a little air in hopes of making the cabin a little more pleasant. That done, I went to work on the engine.

I was only able to run the engine for 1 hour in the last month. An old Perkins 4-108, she doesn't like the cold, and trying to force her to start when the temperature is below 60 degrees was a chore. I had just about killed my batteries by undercharging them over the months in the Southern Ocean. The solar panels couldn't keep up under the constant cloud cover and fog. That day, they were working well in the bright sun and the volt meter rose. I wanted to give the engine one shot. First, I bled the fuel system to make sure she would have fuel from the first press of the start button. Spraying WD-40 into the air intake, I whispered "Come on now, just this once," and held the start button. 2 seconds, 5 seconds, 10 seconds, nothing. Resisting the urge to give it another go, I looked at the volt meter and the electricity that I had lost in those quick seconds. Another day perhaps. I let the solar panels go to work, for I had food in the fridge and couldn't waste any of the precious power.

In the weeks leading up to the food drop off of Port Stanley I watched as my batteries struggled for life. The only load I was putting on the batteries was the AIS. No Nav lights at night or cabin lights, I was down to just the essentials. Nevertheless, I would see the volts go up to about 13 during the day and down to 10 by morning. By all accounts totally flat. And now with the extra load of the fridge, it was going to be tough to keep my precious food from rotting away. I would run the fridge during the day and turn it off at night, trying my best not to open the lid more than absolutely necessary; easier said than done when dealing with a half-starved sailor!

With Sparrow sorted for the moment it was my turn. I wanted to get all of the effort out of the way and work up a good sweat before taking my shower. Striping down in the afternoon, I first noticed the veins on my arms, bulging from my shoulders to my wrists. My arms had turned to twigs with small but very defined muscles. Then I saw the veins that were all over my legs and running up above my waist! "I never had those before! And wait, I have an 8-pack!" I was seeing a different person. In the last two months I had lost every bit of fat and most of my muscle mass. At the beginning of the voyage I had rounded out to about 195 pounds on a diet of beer and junk food. Now I was looking at a body that couldn't have weighed more than 145!

After watching the brownish yellow water run off my body and into the cockpit scuppers, I realized that what I thought was a bit of a tan was just dirt and dead skin. I was white as a ghost and skinny as a skeleton. A handful of cookies and a rum drink followed. This led to a photo shoot on the foredeck, laughing at myself and generally just being able to enjoy the day. All the stresses of Cape Horn and the trip to the Falkland Islands were fading fast. We were now on our way North. Still floating at 49 degrees South latitude, I was nowhere near free of the Southern Ocean. But on this day, I let my worries fade into the setting sun.

Chapter 44
Get me out of here!

I suppose the same feelings fall over all sailors who round Cape Horn and start their way North. I was overwhelmed with relief from slipping by unscathed, but it wasn't long before the cold realization of our position slapped me in the face. As the next weather system approached from the West it brought the normal wind shifts with it. The only difference was we wanted to now head North instead of East.

The wind built to F-6 from the North on April 14th. By noon we had only made 45 miles in 24 hours and were trying to claw our way up wind. We also were fighting an opposing current, so the next 24 hours didn't look good at all. The waves built up to a point that it was impossible to do anything but go Hove-to and wait for the winds to back around to the West. The pounding we were taking was terrible. Midway through changing from the 2nd to 3rd reef, I broke another winch from the boom. Not looking forward to making that repair again, I simply used the repaired winch and stowed the broken one. Even though Sparrow was sailing between 1-3 knots she was launching off the crest of each wave and dropping like a rock down into the following trough.

Each squall brought with it hail in the 40-degree air. When I changed sails, it was necessary to wear my ski goggles and work fast. My bare hands were red and raw each time I returned to the cabin to warm them over the stove. I had a new resolve with our North heading and wanted to get every mile I could. The goal now was to get out of the Southern Ocean and into the Variables before getting smashed by one of the South Atlantic's notoriously violent storms.

While not able to gain any real miles to the North, I focused on following the sun with my solar panels. Heading West in the mornings and back to the East in the afternoon. This kept the charge going on the batteries and allowed me to run the fridge at full tilt. Preserving my precious meats, cheese and bread were a top priority, next to not sinking! The daily run on April 15th was a meager 25 miles and the pressure was dropping fast.

Wind and waves built for the next 24 hours from the North North West. We were pinned down as if the Southern Ocean just wanted to have another go at knocking us around. Some of the most confused seas were being created as the winds backed around the compass. The pressure steadied at 986 as the gale filled in and strengthened from the West. We must have been in an opposing current, as the waves were averaging 20 feet with great breaking crests. The only difference from the last few months was that we were trying desperately to go into the weather. A big change from running with a gale, fore-reaching and even being Hove-to, we really felt the unrelenting power of the sea.

The morning check on deck was a miserable, wet affair but had to be done. Clinging to every hand hold and being covered by the splash of every wave I was able to spot a tiny split pin on deck. Never a good sign. I investigated every pin I could until I found the missing piece. It was the gooseneck. Quickly replacing the split pin, I doubled my efforts to find other problems. Sparrow was tough but she had been through so much, I felt badly that we were having to beat to weather for so long in such bad conditions.

-April 16th 2018 Journal:
The only good thing that came from today was a half-drunk

nap. Beating into this crap is bad. Now 1800, have had to go Hove-to as the pounding was too much at only 2 ½ knots. I hate this. The wind howls and shakes the rig, Sparrow is heeling way over and we take a big wave hit every so often. Can't get a forecast until Sparrow settles so I have no idea how long or how bad it will get. I am so tired of being on the edge. My nerves are shot and I can only sit and wait and hope that Sparrow holds together.-

Times were hard deep in the South Atlantic, but I did have food and six bottles of booze. I was either falling asleep from overeating or from overindulging. I didn't care. Life was very uncomfortable and would be it seemed for many days to come. Three gales in 5 days and two were a bit over the top. Soon the winds did change, and as so many times before, we had made it through the tough times with very little damage.

Our heading was to the North North East as best we could. We needed to get a good bit of Easting in before hitting the South East Trade winds. I wanted nothing more than to be able to power reach once we found them, and that meant getting out away from South America. I was finding that the seas would calm much faster than in the Pacific. Rather than always having the South West swell rolling under us, the seas would calm shortly after the winds. This was something I had been dreaming about for all the months spent sailing in the never-ending fetch of the Southern Ocean. I was starting to see the light at the end of the tunnel.

The night sky was really showing off as well. Night after night, just after sunset, the crescent moon hung under the constellation Orion as Jupiter rose to the East. My old friends had returned, and I looked forward to the coming warmth as we sailed North. With a good supply of coffee, I planned to spend many nights studying the stars of the Southern sky before they disappeared in our wake.

Chapter 45
A Fond Farewell

The beating continued. I slept, ate, and drank my way through 10 days of winds predominantly coming from the North. Just after midnight on April 25th we crossed the 40th parallel and officially made our exit from the Southern Ocean. It was a great day with many drinks and celebrations. Almost as a parting gift, the skies opened up with a heavy downpour. Within 4 hours I had collected nearly 50 gallons of fresh water. The 5-gallon jugs filled so fast I could barely keep up! By the time I emptied one into the main tank the next jug would be overflowing, a truly wonderful problem to have! It was mid-December when we first dipped below 40 degrees South latitude, a long time to spend in the Southern Ocean. One last low-pressure system was tracking to come up from the South but it looked as though I would outrun it and only get the Westerly winds of the North edge of the storm.

Like so many times before, we lay motionless except for the never-ending roll of Sparrow. The sea was noticeably warmer, and to pass the time I decided to give scraping the hull a go. Digging around for a while I finally found my snorkel, mask and fins. I then tied a paint scrapper and brush onto a tether line. Though Sparrow had no sail up and was seemingly standing still, I ran a line overboard from the bow that dangled the full length of the hull. From past experience I knew that a boat always moves in the water; I am not sure how, but it always moves.

A quick look to see if anything big was swimming around, and then another, longer look, just to be sure. I never really like swimming in the open ocean but we were going to need every bit of speed we could get in the coming months of light winds. Over I went and by Neptune we were covered! It was a miracle we could even move with the number of goosenecks hanging off of Sparrow. The little bastards came off quickly and in big clumps. The work was made difficult by the rolling and in about 20 minutes I was very tired. While working hard on the rudder, Sparrow pitched over and gave me a knock on the head, hard enough for me to see a small cloud of blood whisking around my face. Ready to use any excuse to call it a day, I tossed the tools on deck and was poised to climb up the whisker stay and onto the boomkin. I had done this a million times before and thought nothing of it. But I failed to consider that I was nowhere near as strong as I once was. Seven months without any real exercise had taken its toll.

The first attempt was not even close. I was too tired from the effort of scrapping. So, I took a moment to relax and recover my strength. As I hung with one arm on Sparrow my mind started to run wild. I had been making a commotion in the water, I had left a trail of scrapped up goosenecks, and I was bleeding. A heathy dose of adrenaline fueled by a shot of fear and I was onboard in a second! I lay on deck catching my breath for a good while before saying aloud, "Not doing that again."

A quick fresh water rinse, some warm clothes and a cocktail in my hand. Not a bad effort, and I had gotten rid of a good amount of the goosenecks. My arm starting to hurt as I patted myself on the back for a job well done, I decided to run the engine for 30 minutes before sunset just to boost the batteries. With the air temperatures now in the high 60's the engine started without trouble. Though I only used the engine for charging, I liked to work the throttle and transmission a few times by shifting into forward and reverse. A little stiff from neglect I pushed her into reverse, and the engine revved and sounded good. Back to neutral, then forward, then bang and the engine died! I had forgotten to take my safety line out of the water.

I went forward and found that the line was so tight it would have to be cut. After cutting the line forward, I was able to use the boat hook to grab the remainder that was now firmly attached to the propeller. I hoped I could tug it loose but nothing budged. I toyed with the idea of just putting the engine in reverse, but that could go very wrong and I didn't want to add to the list of stupid things I had done in the last hour. With a sigh and a big drink from my cocktail, I striped down, put goggles on and grabbed my filet knife. Over I went again, this time in the fading twilight.

Careful not to cut my fingers off with the extremely sharp blade, I first cut the majority of the line free and went to work on the 4 or 5 wraps that held fast to the propeller shaft. Not easy in the fading light, I couldn't believe I was back in the water. With the job done in just a few minutes I was back on deck and rinsing with fresh water once again. Glad that no one saw how stupid I had been, I mixed a much stronger drink and the world seemed right again. The only thing I could do was to laugh at my own mistake.

The pressure took a steep dive, and by 0200 on May 1st the winds were reaching gale force from the West North West. I hadn't out run anything. The waves grew so quickly that I was shocked. Before the sunrise Sparrow had clocked her all-time highest boat speed of 20.9 knots. We were surfing almost out of control. I didn't care. I wanted every mile we could get. The temperature was already in the high 60's and I wanted more. We pushed on with just the 3rd reef in the mainsail. All night we surfed over and over. I never slept a second with the vibration so loud from the hull and the rigging.

The morning light gave me an idea of just how steep the waves had become. Though the winds had eased off a bit to F-7 the seas were steep and breaking. Looking up the mast at the Windex I noticed it was loose and rocking back and forth. Used for showing the wind direction, I hoped it would stay in place long enough for the seas to calm and me to repair whatever had come loose on its mount. At some point during the day it had given up the fight and was gone. After countless gales and over half of the world's oceans, that little wind arrow had kept its perch atop the mast. "Three cheers for the Windex!" "May you rest in peace!"

The following evening our world had changed. The temperature was holding in the low 70's both day and night. The seas had turned from breaking waves into a rolling swell from the South South West and the winds were down to F-4 and steady. The sun was giving us a good show as it dipped down to the horizon. Great rays of orange and red filled the sky, and for whatever reason, I lost control of my emotions. I don't know if it was the gale or how exhausted I was or maybe just the feeling of having weathered our last Southern Ocean blow. Either way, a great relief flowed forth as we sailed North and back to safety.

Chapter 46
Taking Stock

The first few days of sailing into the Variables were filled with good yet inconsistent winds. It wasn't until May 6th that the daily runs dipped below 120 miles. But we were closing in on the South East Trades and in a good position to ride them all the way to the equator. At 27 degrees South latitude by 29 degrees West longitude Sparrow and I were only a day away from crossing our outbound track, and thus will have circumnavigated Antarctica! It was amazing to look back on the charts; I was overwhelmed by how far we had come.

With just over 24,000 miles sailed so far, we were still a long way from home. At least another 5,000 miles. I had put back some of the weight I had lost, and it was time to take account of all the supplies I had left. More than anything I just wanted to avoid rationing food again.

I had eaten every bit of chocolate and every cookie brought on board in the Falkland's. My growling belly was testament to that! I was back to mostly the staples of canned food, rice, oatmeal, and pasta. The meat and cheese were unfortunately gone. Although I ate with abandon, it was the lack of power from the fridge that did them in. I only had to toss overboard about 1 pound of meat, but wasted at least 5 pounds of cheese. Too much mold had grown, and besides that, the smell of stinking cheese was more than I could put up with. The one drawback from the supplies brought from the Falkland's was the peanut butter. I had asked for 6 large jars. What I received were 6 jars that wouldn't have filled one large American jar! I guess peanut butter and jelly sandwiches really are an American delicacy. All in all, I had plenty of food to go the distance.

The fresh water supply was holding well. With the rain between gales and the constant squalls in the variables I had just about 50 gallons of fresh water aboard. I knew to be as frugal as possible. Once we enter the trades the chances were that we wouldn't see rain until the Doldrums. As for the other drinks aboard, with the gales and the calms I drank every drop to get me through, and for the second time under my watch, the Mighty Sparrow was a dry boat. Not to worry, as I knew a few islands along the way that make some very fine rum!

All else aboard ship was looking fine and working well. Sparrow was in good shape; her sails were a different story. The big drifter was showing more holes every time she flew. I can't be sure, but I think it was an original sail from the 1970's. The heavy mainsail was changed out for the old one after sewing new telltales along the leach. The staysail was only showing wear from when it was lashed to the non-skid deck during heavy weather. The #3 jib needed to be patched every so often but was holding together and showing no signs of blowing out. With the constant sail changes in the variable winds, I had plenty of opportunities to look over each sail once it flew. Many times it came right back down for a bit of sail tape or a trip to the sewing machine.

My first round of laundry was attempted on May 7th when a red sky in the morning turned into a rain filled day. I was able to catch enough to shower and rinse the salt from the laundered clothes. After soaking and agitating my clothes in detergent and salt water I was able to just leave them on deck for the rain to rinse them clean. The rain was clean, but the runoff from the clothes was first brown then yellow and then almost clear. My moldy pillow took much more effort. Each time I rung it out the water was brown. After 7 or 8 rinses, it was still yellow but I figured that was good enough. Once the rains had stopped everything was hung high in the rigging, and though I lost a few socks to the wind, most came back down dry, salt free, and smelling fresh! Never again would I take for granted the ease of a modern washer and dryer. To do one load of laundry aboard Sparrow took not only the right weather conditions but almost an entire day from start to finish.

At 1600 we had officially crossed our outbound track and the ceremony was underway. A different feeling to all the times before as today marked a big accomplishment. A complete circle around Antarctica! I still couldn't believe it. The winds were holding out of the South East and I whispered to myself, "Could I have found the Trades?" By 0130 we were becalmed with no sails flying. But the stars were bright, and we gently rolled. I slept through the rest of the night until morning. Life was calm and relaxing and no longer were we in a hurry to be anywhere.

Chapter 47
My Shangri-La

It seems funny to say but I love light wind sailing. When I think of the perfect sailing conditions, it would be a 12-knot wind on the beam with a following swell just to get the occasional boost in speed. When the open ocean delivers this kind of sailing, I am in heaven. The portholes open to leeward, cooking, sleeping, and reading fill my days and star-gazing fills the night. These were the conditions as the South East Trades filled in on May 8th at just about 25 degrees South latitude.

What made this time even better for me was the length I had to go to finally reach this place. All of the hardships and scary moments in the Great South. Months spent looking over my shoulder and wondering if the next gale would be the big one. The snow and hail squalls. The hunger and depleted water supply. All that suffering helped to make my time in the Trades that much better. The sea was no longer a threat, it was a warm and friendly place. The clouds rolled by without any squalls and the sails stayed full for days on end.

In the mornings I would almost always find flying fish on the deck and cook them for breakfast. One morning I had 4 that were over 6 inches long. It was a grand breakfast. The fishing line was always out. I had started to make my own lures out of old beer cans and they worked well. Mahi Mahi couldn't resist the sparkling shapes that I made and I was eating well. The

Jerome

spinner dolphins came and went as they pleased and I would lay on the bow-sprit and watch. Dangling just a few feet above them I could swear they would give me a wink every so often.

I went to work on weaving a net on the Leeward side of the pulpit so I could relax with the sound of Sparrow's hull parting the sea. I spent as much time as I could on deck just looking out at the beautiful world around me. This was my reward for pushing on and facing the fears I had in the Southern Ocean. All that time stuck down below in the damp, cold cabin was over and now it was my turn to be on deck in the sun. The miles were falling away as well.

Once we reached the Trades the daily runs were 125, 103, 138, 139, 119, 100, 140 147, 129, 140, 128, 118, and 120. Simply great sailing with very little stress. Large clouds came in from the East on May 13th and the rest of the laundry came on deck. I wanted to get all of the cold weather thermals cleaned and stowed as I wouldn't need them for a long time to come. I had also found a bag of wet clothes that I had stowed in the forepeak back in the Indian Ocean. I could feel they were damp and had been so for many months. When I opened the bag, the smell was unbelievable. Some sort of chemical reaction must have happened as the fumes stung my nose like ammonia. Had they been made of cotton I am sure they would have gone overboard, but they were synthetic and one of the tee shirts was my favorite, so they joined the rest of the clothes!

Using salt-water to wash clothes is not as bad as it may seem. The drying process is the important part. I would use normal detergent in a bucket with salt water and then rinse the clothes on deck in the rain. The only problem was that on this day, what I though was a guaranteed rain passed us by and left me with only salt water to rinse with. Once again I turned to the books of the cruising sailors in the 1960's. As long as I could hang everything high in the rig and give them plenty of time to flap in the breeze, the salt crystals would be flicked away and the clothes would be dry and clean. My over-confidence in the rain left me with a bigger pile of clothes than I had clothes pins to hang them! Not to worry. I ran lines through the clothes and soon Mighty Sparrow looked like a laundry boat. A spiderweb of hanging socks, boxers, and thermals from stem to stern all dripping but also filling the air with that clean laundry smell.

Down below, the fight to rid Sparrow of her forest of mold was well underway. I had one bottle of a lemon cleaning spray and an old rag. Getting into as many places as I could I was shocked to see the extent of the growth. The worst areas were inside of the wood cabinet doors. Completely covered with an almost moss-like coat of black and grey mold. I wanted nothing more than to get every last bit, but I settled for making the cabin look and feel clean. The deep clean would come later. As the days fell away in Sparrow's wake, the cabin became more comfortable and more like my home once again.

Probably the best part of sailing in the Trades was being on the starboard tack. I had been thinking about how absolutely wonderful it was going to be to have my bunk on the low side and free of the lee cloth. A multitude of pillows, now clean, adorned my little bed. No longer did I have to climb over the lee cloth and try my best to get comfortable. I could just hop into bed and fall asleep, or read, or just look at the ceiling that was now covered with flags. I still had 3 unread books that I had saved for the long days of sailing North.

With the calm conditions, the sextant came out of hiding and we went back to the days of old for no other reason than having another activity to fill the day. I have always enjoyed the independence that celestial navigation provides. Needing nothing more than a sextant, nautical almanac, clock, and charts, a sailor can pinpoint their position with just the sun. As the excitement of easy sailing and my new comfortable world began to fade, I would need all the distractions I could find to keep my mind occupied. As much as I loved being at sea, after 230 days alone it was just about time to get back to land.

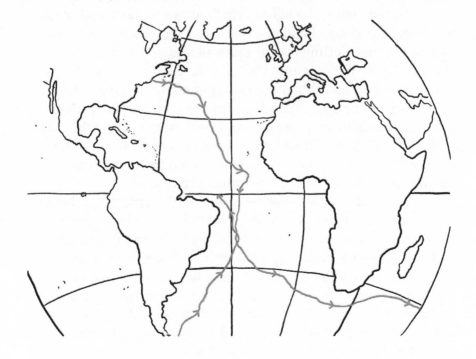

Chapter 48 ✓
Great Expectations

The first sign that I was getting close to the Doldrums were the ships passing from Africa to Panama and the United States. Every day I saw more and more. One night I saw only a red light in the distance. Nothing was on the AIS and I couldn't raise anyone on the VHF. As we sailed closer, I could see that it was actually 2 red lights, one on top of the other. The sign of a vessel "Not under Command." A dark night with no moon hid what I was looking at until we were less than a mile away. It was an oil tanker. At least 800 feet long and from what I could surmise, it was just drifting a few hundred miles off the coast of Brazil. Everything was blacked out and no other lights but the double red were on. I could smell exhaust as we passed down wind but there were no other signs of life at all. I dubbed it the Ghost Ship and sailed away, I did toy with the idea of sailing in close and seeing if I could take her as salvage. The image of Sparrow towing an 800-foot tanker into Gloucester made me laugh out loud!

The winds had dropped off by May 20th and I knew we had entered the Doldrums once more. I did, however, have it in my head that we were going to fly right by. Six months ago, we had a tough go with all of the fearsome squalls and dead calms. But my reading in books about the world cruising routes told of an easier passage through the Doldrums the closer one sails to Brazil, as opposed to the African Coast. I expected a few days of floating around and dealing with squalls. I had no idea just how bad it was going to get.

The sun beat down with unrelenting strength. With temperatures in the high 80's and low 90's all movements slowed way down. As we passed the equator the daily runs dropped right off. First 66 miles then 46 and again down to 26. The flags went up and the ceremony was joyous, but as the flags hung limp on the halyard, they seemed to mock me! On the 24th we had only moved .8 of a mile in 24 hours! I didn't even think it was possible to sit in one place in the ocean for that long. Nevertheless we had our slowest 24 hour run of the trip.

What made my dive into the Doldrums so hard was the constant need to take advantage of every puff of wind that came our way. The sails went up and down constantly. Playing the game of having too much sail up as a squall approached and then changing sail quickly to squeeze out every inch was all I could do. 24 hours a day I worked to crawl North at an average speed of 1.4 knots. Just when I thought we might be breaking free, the winds would die and we drifted like a sitting duck.

One morning the AIS alarm woke me from a dead sleep.

880 feet of steel was heading right for us at 13 knots. On deck I could only see the white superstructure of the ship's bridge at first. Between the binoculars and the AIS I could see we were on a collision course, or at least they were. Sparrow and I were just floating, no sails up and no wind to catch. We also had no engine to use. I had run out of fuel weeks before and cursed myself for not holding onto a few gallons for emergency maneuvers! Calling on the VHF was fruitless and after a few unanswered calls I gave up. The ship, now only two miles away, was still heading right for us! I did what I thought might help, and that was to raise the colorful spinnaker. Green, yellow and orange filled the rigging, and at least we were a little more visible. Back and forth between the Nav station and the binoculars, I was starting to get very worried. I could only imagine sailing so far just to have a tanker run us down in the Doldrums!

I am not sure if they noticed me eventually, or it was just dumb luck, but the ship passed at a very uncomfortable distance of only 200 yards. The vibrations of the tanker's engines shook Sparrows rigging and could be felt as well as heard. I miss the days when I first ventured out on the ocean 15 years ago. Things have definitely changed. Long gone are the days when ships at sea would pause and chat as fellow ocean travelers. I guess the world just doesn't have time for that kind of thing anymore.

Three days in a row, each with a daily run of less than 40 miles, took their toll on my mind. I had rigged a windchime in the cockpit to wake me if the slightest breeze came up. I needed to take advantage of every puff no matter what time of day or night. The small island of Sao Paulo was less than 60 miles to the North East when I started to see fishing buoys and strobe lights through the night. One little boat came over the horizon, heading South, at least when I first spotted her.

Anytime I sighted another boat at sea I would always watch it. Not only to make sure we would pass safely but also just to stare at something besides the sea and sky. As I watched, this little ship changed its heading and looked as though it was coming our way. Not giving it much thought, I went below to see what info I could get about it on the AIS. Nothing. I always figured that fishing boats would turn off their AIS as to not give away their precious fishing spots. A look back on deck and the little ship had closed the distance and was still heading right for us. Not fast, and still a few miles away, I was beginning to make out some detail with the help of the binoculars. The first thought that came to mind was the amount of rust all over the bow. I guested she was about 70 feet and couldn't see any form of fishing gear, just a dirty old ship heading right for me.

In the middle of the ocean it is very uncommon, at least in my experience, to have a vessel change course and approach without at least a call on the VHF. I was getting nervous as she slowly closed the gap. I watched with growing awareness that we were about to have our first unannounced visitor of the trip. As my mind raced and heart pounded, all I could think was pirates! I had the shotgun but it wasn't loaded; "Should I load it?" Maybe I would pull the move from the old books; go below and change clothes and pop out from the forward hatch to make it seem that I wasn't alone. All the while the little ship approached. It should be mentioned that the winds were blowing at about F-2 and Sparrow was moving at a steady 3 knots. Similar to the incident with the tanker, we were a sitting duck.

I gave up all hope of fending off an attack as the Ship was now only a few hundred yards off our beam. I could do nothing but sit and wait to see what they were going to do. At the very last minute, about 100 feet from Sparrow, the ship turned 90 degrees and slowed. Five smiling faces were standing at the stern rail, with two fishermen holding what had to have been the cleaned remains of a 100-pound tuna. "Buy Fish, buy fish?" They shouted. I had to pick my heart up off the cabin sole before I could answer with an "all good" and a wave of no thanks. The relief flooded into me as the adrenaline faded away. I was tempted to wave them back and buy the fish, or at least maybe see if they had a smaller one, but the thought of getting holed as they tried to motor close to Sparrow didn't seem worth the risk. The lessons of the circumnavigators of old were still ringing in my ears and I was happy to listen.

The days rolled on, one after another, with little to no wind at all. More rivet heads were found on the deck and a look up the mast track showed the damage. No longer straight and true, the track had bends and bulges where the slides were exerting the most force as the mainsail slammed from one side to the other. I couldn't keep the mainsail up. I had to except that I was either sailing or drifting, and nothing in between. The sails take a beating in the light conditions as much as any gale. One dark night I was dead asleep with every stich of canvas flying when Sparrow lurched over and with a loud bang, she started to shudder like crazy. In the half-light I could see that the big drifter was already shredded to pieces! My favorite light wind sail was dying! Quick on deck to lower the sail I took pause, as I knew I was too late. The damage done and the squall over as fast as it came on, Sparrow's biggest wing was now broken beyond repair. Though the sail was old it had seen me through so many calms, and kept Sparrow moving along many a glassy sea. It was my fault for leaving it up through the night and I guess I was just lucky nothing else broke in the squall.

In the light of day, I could see that the sudden impact of the wind had done some damage to the bow sprit. Made of three pieces of wood glued and bolted together, the bow sprit had started to come apart. I wondered just how much it bent in the blow. In the calm conditions, it was an easy fix with some epoxy and a few clamps. I would have to keep an eye on the repair and be a little more cautious with the big headsails exerting too much pressure on the bowsprit.

By May 29th I was reaching the end of my patience for the Doldrums. Another daily run of 50 miles, our 9th day in a row of very low numbers. I began cursing the North East Trade for not showing up sooner. So much for the guide books with all the promises of a narrow crossing closer to Brazil! We were floating amongst a large patch of seaweed so flat and becalmed I could see the Mahi swimming around. So brilliant with the green and blue skin, more like a reef fish than an ocean predator. I followed my new friends around with the fishing line in a weak attempt to get lucky when I started to hear a sound. Almost like a waterfall. Not the sound of wind but the sound of many waves crashing on a beach. I couldn't see anything on the sea or in the sky but the sound was getting louder. For the next 30 minutes I listened, watched, and waited. The sky was overcast and the day coated in the dull grey light. One minute we were floating with no sails up, and in the next I was scrambling to raise the mainsail. I had found the North East Trades!

As if a switch went from "Off to On" we were soon sailing at 6-7 knots on a shallow broad reach in a perfect 15 knot wind. Try as it might, the Doldrums couldn't keep Sparrow from breaking free of its all-powerful grip. We had entered the final ocean on the voyage, the North Atlantic. I was frazzled for sure. The Doldrums had taken a big toll both physically and mentally. Sparrow was a bit beat up and showing more wear each day. The two of us relying on the other. One more ocean, one more month. I am sure we both wondered if the other would hold together.

Chapter 49
An Endless Coast

Well into the North East Trade winds by the 1st of June, we continued to romp our way directly for the heart of the Caribbean. The sailing was easy. I first toyed with combinations of the mainsail and different headsails but soon found that I could manage the same boat speed with just the small drifter. One or two squalls would come in every day but never too violent. Instead of changing sail, I would give Mongo a break and helm right through. Our determination showed in the daily runs, almost all of which were over 150 miles per day!

Everything seemed to stay the same. We were going to be sailing parallel to the coast of Brazil about 500 miles offshore for nearly two weeks. The winds held between F-4 and 5. The barometer only moved a few bars a day, 1000 to 1008, never more or less. We were in one of the greatest wind belts on the planet; one could almost sleep for days at a time without worry of falling off course. It was truly a time to "set it and forget it."

Huge areas of seaweed ran in strips along the ocean surface and were plowed right through. The sound sometimes scared me at night, and sometimes the seaweed would get caught on Mongo's rudder. Just about the only excitement aboard Sparrow. I would have to go and dangle off the boomkin with a broom stick and try my best to remove the seaweed, as it dulled Mongo's ability to keep a good heading. We were moving so fast that it was very difficult to hold myself and the stick at the same time. I would poke and prod and finally the weed would fall away. The Mahi Mahi were everywhere around the seaweed as well. I could see them chasing the flying fish. If I caught sight of one, I would send my beer can lure over. On one try I spotted the fish, put the line out and then had him aboard in less than a minute! By now I was looking for anything to add to my diet. The flying fish helped in that regard as well. Day or night, if I heard the welcome sound of a constant thumping on deck, I knew it was snack time. Easy to clean and quick to fry I would sometimes wake from a deep sleep to the thump. Like an automated machine, I would grab the cutting board and knife and head to the cockpit. Soon the smell of frying fish would fill the air and after no more than 20 minutes I was back in my bunk. Sparrow, it turns out, was a great fishing net, and I was the mindless eating machine that lived below her deck.

Day after day nothing changed. I read all but one of my books and listened to the podcasts and audio books that I had heard many times before. It was a comfort to have a voice besides mine on board; the more I listened the more I started to depend on them. I would use the little World Band Radio if the night was clear. Searching for hours I would sometimes find the news from the BBC or Voice of America. I wasn't particularly interested in the news, what I wanted was new voices and new content whatever it might be. I was finding myself in a depth of loneliness that I had yet to experience on the voyage. For the first months of the trip I was facing a daunting challenge, the Southern Ocean and the 5 Great Southern Capes. With the physical challenges of that part over, I was left with a possibly much more difficult obstacle; my own isolation.

I had read about sailors reaching a point where they could stay happy alone at sea conceivably forever. Once they had been out for over 200 days or so. I had also read stories of the ones who never came back, or who made it back but were never the same. How many times could I check the rigging, clean the cabin, or listen to a story or song? My body wouldn't let me sleep 12 hours a day and I had nothing but the familiar all around me. 32 feet by 11 feet, my tiny world surrounded by infinity. As the days rolled on, I fought to keep my mind from focusing on time. My only escape was to cast off the rules I had set. I let my mind wander into the future more and more.

My favorite thoughts were of the woods at home in Michigan. That was where I was going to set up camp for the summer. I knew already that I would have trouble locking myself into four walls, unable to hear the wind. I wanted to carry on living outside and dealing with the elements. I plotted and planned down to every last detail what my camp would look like. Luck just had it that I had taken two pictures of an area of forest that I could use for my new home. I suppose it gave me a little comfort that my life wouldn't change too much after returning to land. I was also starting to wonder about what it was really going to be like to make the adjustment back to a normal life. One thing for sure, as we sailed closer to the Caribbean, my head was spinning. I needed change and I needed a distraction. I would have to settle for rum, lots of rum!

A few days out from Dominica the sands of the Sahara Desert filled the air. So thick that it was covering the windward side of all the lines with a red brown coat. The sails stayed clean except for the stitching. They looked more like Frankenstein with all the repairs contrasting with the white of the sails. I looked on like a proud father at the work I had done, but also marveled that the work had held for so long. I hoped the sails would go the distance without the aid of the sewing machine. I had received word from a great friend from Dominica that he would be in Portsmouth and would come say hello. And most definitely bring rum!

By June 7th the winds had come around right out of the East and we were heading due West to the North end of Dominica. The winds were too strong for the spinnaker, so the mainsail was eased, and the jib poled out. We rolled during the day and we rolled at night. 30 degrees on each side. Sleeping was becoming more difficult and moving around required all hands to keep from losing my footing. Worse yet, I had developed the most unbelievable case of gas in my life. Not only was it constant but it produced an odor that was impossible to describe. Either I went on deck when I had the urge or once released the smell drove me out like smoke in a bee hive. Something was definitely going on inside my body.

Winds and rain filled the sky as we passed the Northern tip of Dominica under a dark night. Strong gusts rolled off the high mountains causing a frantic change of sails as we rounded the island and entered the Caribbean Sea. Like being in my backyard, I felt at home. I knew this place well and even in the dark I found an area to Hove-to to get some rest. It was only an hour or so before the sun would be up but that was all I needed.

I woke to a flat calm. The lee of mountains over 4,000 feet high. I thought I might get lucky and catch some of the famous Dominican rain, but it was clear skies the whole time. Tacking back and forth, I had no idea when I would see my friends. After 251 days alone with only Sparrow and Mongo to talk to, I was about to see people, not only people but old friends! Portsmouth is over a mile wide and a perfect bay for sailing. Deep water all around without any worry of hitting bottom. I hadn't seen land so close since the Snares and I let it envelope me. The green was so striking, and all the little fishing boats that passed by waved and smiled. One of my favorite Caribbean islands, Dominica is truly a friendly place.

My friends came through! They handed over boxes of rum and beer and snacks for my trip North. It was with eager hands that I took possession. I often wonder what they were thinking looking back at me. Who is this strange bearded man that looked like Jerome? The minutes flew by and before I knew it, we were setting sail and waving goodbye. At noon I was clear of Dominica and on a heading for Virgin Gorda in the British Virgin Islands. I was making good on a promise to sail by the Bitter End Yacht Club and see more friends. Just over 230 miles to the North West and I had sailed those miles many times before.

Sailing fast with a cold beer in hand, the first since Cape Horn, the winds were strong and Sparrow was plowing through the sea as steady as a rock. As we approached the calm that is ever-present in the lee of Guadalupe, the winds went light but I wasn't in the mood to slow down. Until then I had never had use for the asymmetrical spinnaker. It was a sail that was great when I had others aboard, but it was old and tired. I figured it might be fun. Pulling the bag from the depths of the forepeak I found the whole thing to be wet and salty. Nevertheless, I raised the sail in its snuffer and unleashed the beast. For all of 30 seconds she filled the sky and we powered right back up. Then it was too much power, and the sail exploded. Either from neglect on the trip or just age, the sail turned to shreds in seconds. I was able to haul everything back on board and set the small drifter in its place. I was soaking wet sitting on the bow covered in torn nylon, laughing all the way. For the first time in a long while I was having fun sailing again.

After far too many beers, I had gone down below for a long sleep. The winds were steady, and Sparrow seemed content to take me back to Virgin Gorda without worry. Flying the small drifter and full mainsail would normally have put a bit of caution in my mind, but I felt overconfident being back in my home waters and I slept deeply. Some hours later, Sparrow had found her way out of the lee of Guadalupe and the winds had filled in. I can't be sure how long we had been screaming along but when the sound of surfing finally woke me, I could feel that things were not right. On deck and rubbing my eyes, I could make out that we were sailing at around 9 knots and surfing small waves that had built up. I had left Sparrow with far too much sail up and though she was holding her own, I could feel that we needed to drop the drifter. Slowly I crawled forward. Releasing the halyard, the line flew through my hand and the crackle of a flogging sail filled my ears. Quick to the bowsprit and gripping with my legs I was able to get the sail down but the majority fell in the sea. The tug of war took about ten minutes, but I finally was able to lash the drifter and set the #3 jib. I was back in the cockpit and cursing myself for drinking too much and risking the completion of the voyage. I was getting sloppy and needed to get my head back in the game. We only had 2,000 miles left to go and plenty of dangers along the way.

Chapter 50
Virgin Gorda and Beyond

Almost 40 hours after leaving Dominica we were sailing past Necker Island and heading into the North Sound on Virgin Gorda. A perfect sailing ground and a place I knew better than anywhere in the world. We sailed through the main channel under the stars. It was amazing to have Sparrow sailing like she was on rails, no rolling or swell. I could walk around the deck without holding on! It was amazing! As the morning light filled the sky, I was given my first view of the devastation that the island had gone through with Hurricane Irma. The Bitter End lay in a pile of rubble and my little cottage home that I loved so much was gone! Nothing but a foundation to mark where I spent three years of my life.

The VHF started calling as soon as I was spotted. A few friends were waiting for me. I sailed Hove-to and doodled around saying hello and just relishing the fact that I could talk to more friends. Soon more came out with gifts of beer and rum. I was going to be well stocked for the trip North for sure. All of the smiling faces and the feeling of being home already made the urge to drop anchor so strong that I knew I needed to get out before I made a big mistake. After almost 6 hours of joyous reunions with friends from my wonderful years spent on Virgin Gorda it was time to head North. The winds were solid from the

East and perfect for heading home.

As we left the island of Anegada in our wake, I was filled with the memories of all the people that I had just seen. I was in a very happy place as the winds eased up a bit and seas became flat. As long as the waves didn't come up, we were able to sail well under full canvas. I had a fridge that was full of cold beer, some new snacks and a decent weather forecast for the coming days. More than at anytime on the voyage I was right where I wanted to be, at sea but confident that we were going to go the distance. My only worry was fresh water, less than 20 gallons left.

After so many weeks since the last time it rained, and being in the warm tropics, the grey cloud of bacteria was coming back and the water tasted funny. I did find my old household water filter and was using it for peace of mind more than function. The filter was very old and I couldn't imagine that it was really doing much to purify the water. On June 18th I started to see red spots all over my arms. I wasn't sure if it had anything to do with the water or maybe the oppressive sun, but within a day they were gone again. My stomach was still upset but being so close to finishing I wasn't too worried.

The winds came around to the South and dropped even more. The only way to keep moving was to change our heading or get the big spinnaker out. I worked to extend the spinnaker pole that I had modified to use with the jib and staysail. Once that was done the big sail went up. Normally, I would never have been able to get Mongo to behave with the spinnaker but for some reason Mongo found the groove. The sail went up around 0600 and didn't come back down until the wind completely died just after sunset. My patience was going to be tested in the coming days.

Our daily runs since leaving the Caribbean were 109, 130, 110, and 80 miles. Not a bad start for the final leg. The next four day were not so good. 40, 62, 47, and 78 miles. I was losing my mind. Working the sails with every puff we were surrounded by large clouds that were reminiscent of the Doldrums. Lightning filled the nights, but the rain never came as the sea turned to glass. The frustration I was feeling replaced all the good that seeing my friends had brought. I was in a terrible mood during the four days of calm.

My dreams were vivid and disturbing. One such dream found me still in the Pacific Ocean and with a friend onboard. My friend had brought his two dogs and we were fighting about what to do as we didn't have enough food to feed them. I was awake for the rest of the night having awoken in pool of sweat, very shaken. One thing was for sure; I had a lot on my mind as we slowly closed in on Gloucester.

Besides the nightmares that plagued me each night I was finding that my stomach was not liking something that I was eating. After a few hours of tossing and turning I would have to go on deck and vomit. I cut out what I thought might be the problem, a few expired cans of tuna. They smelled and tasted fine, but I didn't want to risk full blown food poisoning. The next night came and the same nausea hit and I was back on deck "feeding the fish." I had barely eaten anything but porridge, rice, and some canned food. All looked and tasted good. I realized it had to be the fresh water.

At this point I only had one tank that still had rain water from the Doldrums in it. A very obvious cloud had grown and when I checked the filters they were clogged with the grey slick. I started to triple filter the water before drinking it and limited myself to a few quarts a day. If it didn't work, I was going to either start boiling the water first, or I had even thought I could go into the life raft and take the water rations. That would be the absolute last resort.

The next night, as we approached the approximate position of the Gulf Stream, I had no issues and my stomach felt much better than it had in weeks. A few large and menacing thunderstorms rolled in and gave us an impressive welcome to this volatile area of the ocean. Large lightning bolts from cloud to sea struck with loud blasts of thunder that followed only a second or two after. Always a scary sight for me, I focused on changing sails and working hard to get Sparrow moving in the building winds.

By noon on June 24th the winds were favorable for crossing the Gulf Stream as they were coming from the South West and blowing between F-5 and 6. The seas erupted from their calm state for the last two weeks and we pounded our way right past in one night, and had made 141 miles by noon the next day. It was a good change for me mentally. The boredom, heat, sickness and long days with low miles had really taken their toll on my morale. Regardless, like so many times before, the calms were in the past and with better sailing my attitude followed suit. I looked forward to smooth sailing for the remainder of the trip.

-June 24th 2018 Journal:
Finally, and thankfully the wind has filled in! I have to say that since the calms set in a week ago, it has been some of the most miserable time aboard Sparrow so far. The heat, the noise, the sickness, and the boredom were taking their toll. I truly didn't know how much more I could take. Very close to my limits. Now we blast North and are less than 500 miles from Gloucester. With good winds we will be in Port by the 30th. Mixed feelings about returning. No more books, no more music, I just spend my days thinking.-

By the next day we must have crossed over into one of the large eddies that border the Gulf Stream, and the seas built fast and became very uncomfortable. To say that I was in a fragile state of mind would be a massive understatement. With every change of the wind or sea my mood would swing from good to bad.

-June 25th 2018 Journal:
Not a fun day at all! I am not doing well. I give up. Reefed down and Hove-to until the sea starts acting like the sea again. One last kick in the teeth? I don't want to lose any more ground so I just have to wait it out.-

We crossed out of the eddy and the seas did calm back

down as fast as they built up. I spotted the first sailboat of the entire trip, outside of the Caribbean. A testament to the emptiness of the offshore world, she looked to be heading to Bermuda. I was glad to be sailing in the other direction and only a few days away from Gloucester. I sighted more and more ships as the day went on into the night. Closing in on Cape Cod and Georges Bank the fishing fleets surrounded us.

The AIS alarm never really stopped beeping and the VHF chatter was constant. As much as I wanted to just turn them off, I knew I couldn't. On deck I could see a few fishing boats within 6 miles at all times. Like a giant game of chicken, I changed my heading many times to avoid and give way to the working ships. Sleep was out of the question, not only from the traffic but from the growing excitement of our imminent landfall. We slipped through the busy shipping lanes that lie off Cape Cod. By the morning of June 29th, we found ourselves in the inky fog that regularly covers Stellwagen Bank.

Sails still up and ghosting along through the fog I could hear the sounds of Humpback Whales in the distance. A cold morning, I was back in my thermals and winter hat. The condensation covered everything and dripped from my beard. Only 35 miles from Eastern Point Break Wall and the finish line. It looked as though I would make it a day before my intended ETA. As the fog was slowly burned away by the sun, so went the whisper of a wind we were riding.

By noon all sails were down and we drifted on a sea that looked like an oil slick. 20 miles from Gloucester, I couldn't see the land but the lobster boats zipped around in the distance all day. After a few hours a beautiful lobster boat, Golden Girl, came by to check and see if everything was ok. After telling the crew that I didn't have any fuel left and just had to wait for the wind, we talked about how long I had been at sea. "270 days out," I said. "You want some food?" they called back. A resounding Yes and they maneuvered close and tossed over a few bottles of water, a fresh pre-made salad, and two BBQ chicken breasts! I received them with shaking hands and many thanks were given. I could have sat and chatted all day but they were working and motored away to leave me to enjoy my unexpected feast alone. I have never eaten a salad so slowly in my entire life! And the chicken was so far beyond good it would be impossible to describe.

A slight breeze picked up and we were able to cut the distance to Gloucester using the spinnaker alone. Whales and dolphins played under the setting sun. A beautiful scene as Cape Ann came into view. We crept closer and closer but it was a lost cause. The wind totally went flat by 2100 just 5 miles out from Gloucester! I would spend another night at sea. I was sad to know that so many friends and family were all so close, having a great night together while I sat just a few miles away.

The lights of shore blazed all around and airplanes circled above on their way to Logan International. A completely different world. A world full of people. The smell of seaweed filled the air and after a long time on deck and a few calls from friends and family I went below to try to sleep.

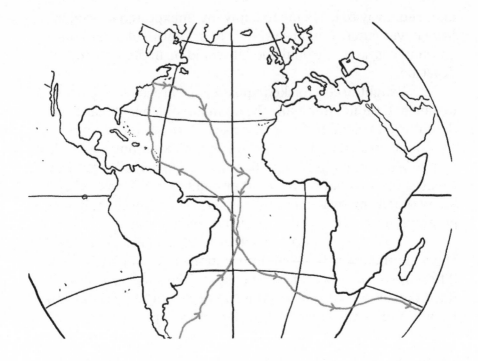

Chapter 51
Landfall Gloucester

Five hours later, as the sky filled with the warm glow from the sun, my cell phone beeped. Mike Porter was on his way and wanted to know where I was! We had drifted about 4 miles to the West and were now just 9 miles due South of Gloucester. A slight breeze came up from the North and so I set sail and started to close the gap. My phone beeped again, this time from my Uncle Bill, he too, was on his way. It was all happening so fast, something I was not used to at all. I then spotted Mike bearing down on us in a 22-foot powerboat.

Alongside and having a great laugh he handed me pizza and a cold beer. The breakfast of champions! The flavors exploded in my mouth and I tried my best to balance talking and eating. We chatted for a while, and as Bill and my parents arrived in another boat Mike went back to Gloucester to pick up more family and friends. Hugs and congratulations abounded. I could see the relief in my Mother's eyes; she didn't have to worry about me anymore! Bill had brought out 5 gallons of fuel and a timeline for the coming day. It was a big day for my Gloucester HQ.

I had been delivered to Gloucester on a very busy weekend. The Greasy Pole, Fiesta, and the Blessing of the Fleet had the Harbor Master abuzz with a full plate and not much time to deal with some "Round the World Sailor." "We have a window of 10-11am to be on the dock and then we have to go," said Bill. Without any wind to speak of, I would have to motor the last 5 miles into Gloucester to make it in time. No complaints from me. I went to work on the engine that I hadn't run in almost two months. First adding the fuel and then bleeding the system. A few unsuccessful tries and then she roared to life! I really didn't want to be towed into Gloucester, and was filled with relief when I shifted into forward and Sparrow began to move.

Flags flying as we motor sailed right for Eastern Point. An hour away, I was once again left alone with Sparrow. As we made our way a few boats came out to greet us. First one, then two and then it seemed like we were surrounded. I tipped my hat to one man who had rowed a small dory all the way out to the finish line. What a feeling! Friends and family all around. Waving and smiling, beers were tossed aboard and I thought I had better ease up or risk falling onto the dock! The last few seconds of the voyage passed by so fast. The break wall and Red buoy were crossed and the Eastern Point Yacht Club cannon rang out. Standing on the bowsprit, I raised my arms and gave a good shout, we had made it! After 271 days and some 29,805 miles, we were finally home.

By 1030 Sparrow was slowly motoring her way to the Harbor Master's Dock. A Coastguard boat escorted us all the way, spouting out a 60-foot fountain from its water cannon. A few more cannon blasts echoed through downtown Gloucester. People cheered from other boats and from shore. I was overwhelmed with joy. After tying up and shutting down the engine, I took my first step onto the dock. At that moment, even though I will probably never know what made me go on the voyage, I knew for sure, I was glad that I went.

The End

In memory of
Arthur Ward Jenks "Buzz"

Epilogue

Though I had been offered a warm bed for my first night ashore, I decided that I couldn't leave Sparrow and cut the bond we had created just yet. I had a crazy night filled with dreams. I woke a few times hurrying to the cockpit not knowing where I was. I figure it was the sounds of downtown Gloucester that played in my head.

After two more days surrounded by friends and family, the last leg of the voyage was underway with my older brother Sven. He had made the heavy weather mainsail and staysail that proved perfect for the trip and would join as my crew on the sail back to Rockland, Maine. A great passage with lots of laughs and Sven filling me in with tales of all the news stories I had missed while out at sea. Becalmed in the night, we motored our way through the islands and onto the dock at Knight Marine Services.

Sparrow was hauled out and given her well-deserved break. I spent a week aboard, mostly cleaning while we both tried our best to adjust to living on land. Sparrow looked good but was showing signs that she was in need of a break. Normally, the bottom would have been pressure washed, but for some reason only a few goosenecks still held fast and were easily scrapped off as they dried out.

I soon shaved off my beard with the possibility of a date. 271 days was a long time to be alone! I had also been feeling like "Father Time" as I walked the streets of Rockland. Still bumping into walls and never able to walk a straight line, I was finding it a challenge to find my land legs. My plan was to head back to Michigan to fulfill a promise to my Mother and be home for the rest of the summer. But not before driving to Gloucester to present the story of my voyage.

Soon I was home and within a few days I had set up my camp in the woods. I built wood platforms for the two large tents and added a solar panel for electricity and even had a water catch system! Once everything was in place, I lay on the woodchips around a crackling fire and stared at the stars peeking through the canopy of leaves. I was finally in the place that I had been dreaming of for all those months at sea. With a smile and a good laugh, I shouted "I made it!"

My time in Michigan after the voyage was great. Surrounded by friends and family I ate and shared stories and had wonderful times. I did find a few things hard to deal with. The most notable was my experience with grocery shopping. I was absolutely overwhelmed. I would walk the seemingly endless isles and stare at all the food. People buzzing around me with full carts while I stood motionless. Trying my best not to talk to myself I would just grab a few things and go. It was too much to take in all at once. But slowly I regained my ability to go about the normal life of a person on land.

It wasn't long before I was searching for something to fill the void in my life. I dubbed my feelings as post adventure depression. Five years had been dedicated to this one goal. Everything I did in that time had a purpose, but what now? As I write these words, all of which have been written while at anchor aboard the Mighty Sparrow in the protection of the islands of Virgin Gorda and Dominica, I gently roll with Sparrow. I know now that this never-ending roll is telling me something. It's Sparrow's way of saying she needs the wind in her sails and is ready to head for the endless horizon once more. All I need to do is point the way.

Glossary

AIS. Automatic Identification System, used aboard vessels to avoid collisions at sea. With the AIS an alarm can be set to alert the presence of another ship nearby.

Beat. The act of sailing a boat into the wind. Most commonly 45 degrees from the wind direction.

Bow Sprit. A pole extended from the forward end of a sailboat used to add additional sail area.

Beam. The side of the boat. The most vulnerable area that can be hit by a large wave.

Dodger. A small canvas cover fitted in the cockpit that offers protection from the wind and sea spray.

Drifter. A very large forward sail for use in light wind conditions

GPS. Global Positioning System, a tool used to keep track of a boats position utilizing a network of satellites.

Hove -To. The act of stalling or stopping a sailboat when at sea. Normally done by arranging the sails to stop forward motion and encourage drifting with the wind while staying in control.

Jibe. When the Mainsail moves quickly from one side of a boat to the other. This is done when sailing with the wind coming from behind the boat.

Knockdown. When a boat is pushed over on its side to 90 degrees or more by either the wind or waves.

Port. When looking forward on a boat the port side is to the left.

Preventer. A line from the end of the boom run forward to stop the Mainsail from an accidental Jibe.

Reach. The act of sailing across or perpendicular to the wind.

Reefing. The act of making a sail smaller in size. Traditionally by lowering the sail a few feet and rolling up the excess. This is done as wind speeds increase.

Run. The act of sailing in the same direction as the wind.

Seacock. A valve that can be opened or closed. Usually located below the waterline in a boat and connected to an opening in the hull.

Spinnaker. A very lightweight and normally large sail used when sailing with the wind.

Squall. A localized wind caused when rain falls from a cloud. As the cold air hits the surface of the sea, the wind is forced outward and can become very violent.

Starboard. When looking forward on a boat the Starboard side is to the Right.

Storm-Jib. A very small and very durable sail used when winds become too strong for normal sails.

Winch. A circular device that is used to manage lines with heavy loads of force. Usually with internal gears and a handle, a winch allows one to gain a mechanical advantage when adjusting sails.

Windvane. A non-electrical self-steering device used to maintain the direction a sailboat will travel. I named mine "Mongo".

ACKNOWLEDGMENTS

This voyage would not have been possible without the help I received from family and friends. Bob and Kathy kept me well fed and got me away from boat preparations when I needed it most. Porkchop with his weather eye and a glorious delivery of pizza the morning of my return. Bill and Jennifer for opening their home in Gloucester. Andy and Tegan for capturing footage of the departure and return to Gloucester, including the cover for this book. Robert who put together a fantastic video of my departure. Nick who sent me off with an envelope full of pictures from home, one for each month at sea. Thank you, Collin, for giving me the honor of spreading the ashes of a true adventurer, Buzz. My brother Sven for building the strongest set of sails I have ever used. My brother Adam for lending his time to help get the boat ready for sea. My Father for being a true inspiration for my life on the ocean. Finally, my Mother for putting up with such a dangerous adventure.

A special thanks to Elizabeth. I am not sure which I appreciate more, your kind words or sharp eye for detail. Either way, thank you so very much.

Made in the USA
Monee, IL
28 May 2021